"*This Is Only a Test* exposes our fears—real and fake, invented and embedded—of disasters. Through Hollars's own experiences, research, and rememberings, he examines how our fears are often unfounded or inflated, even created. B. J. Hollars is in a field all of his own."

—Jill Talbot, author of *The Way We Weren't: A Memoir*

"Through spare, haunting, and heart-wrenching prose, Hollars deftly guides the reader from the tornado-torn streets of Tuscaloosa to the lakes and rivers of Wisconsin, from his backyard to nuclear Japan, and ultimately into those tiny intimate moments of fear that shape a new father's consciousness. Combining a novelist's ear for dialogue and drama with a poet's eye for detail, Hollars's essays delve into the hard spaces, mapping out a place for hope, or at least some small moments of happiness."

—Steven Church, author of *Ultrasonic: Essays*

"In these quirky, inventive stories, B. J. Hollars depicts a world both dangerous and unreasonable, a place where the local TV meteorologist assumes the quality of a god. Character may not be fate in *This Is Only A Test* but the reverse is always true—we reveal ourselves by our response to the random cruelties of the universe, from errant meteor strikes to a small child's fever rising in the night."

—John Hildebrand, author of
The Heart of Things: A Midwestern Almanac

THIS IS ONLY A TEST

break away books

Michael Martone

THIS
IS
ONLY
A
TEST

B. J. Hollars

INDIANA UNIVERSITY PRESS

Bloomington & Indianapolis

This book is a publication of

Indiana University Press
Office of Scholarly Publishing
Herman B Wells Library 350
1320 East 10th Street
Bloomington, Indiana 47405 USA

iupress.indiana.edu

The paper used in this publication
meets the minimum requirements of
the American National Standard for
Information Sciences—Permanence
of Paper for Printed Library
Materials, ANSI Z39.48–1992.

*Manufactured in the
United States of America*

*Library of Congress
Cataloging-in-Publication Data*

Hollars, B. J.
  [Short stories. Selections]
  This is only a test / B. J. Hollars.
    pages ; cm.— (Break Away Books)
  ISBN 978-0-253-01817-5
(softcover : acid-free paper)—ISBN
978-0-253-01821-2 (ebook)
    I. Title.
  PS3608.O48456A6 2016
  813'.6—dc23

                          2015013860

1 2 3 4 5   21 20 19 18 17 16

To Meredith, Henry, and Eleanor,
who always allow me to retake the test.

I came to explore the wreck.
The words are purposes.
The words are maps.

ADRIENNE RICH, "Diving into the Wreck"

CONTENTS

ACKNOWLEDGMENTS

Writing a book, like enduring a disaster, requires all hands on deck.
And so a warm thank-you goes out to my family, friends, and supporters who have often manned the buckets to keep this ship afloat.

Additional thanks go to the editors who have previously published these works, including Nik De Dominic, Marcel Savino, W. Scott Olsen, Steven Church, Karen Craigo, Cory Aarland, Adam Kullberg, Roxane Gay, S. L. Weisenberg, Dan Wickett, Matthew Gavin Frank, Dinty W. Moore, Shena McAuliffe, Adam Weinstein, Kim Groninga, Anjali Sachdeva, Sam Martone, Jeff Albers, and Allegra Hyde.

Thanks to Walter Font of the Allen County–Fort Wayne Historical Society for his additional fact-checking as well.

Thank you to my colleagues at the University of Wisconsin–Eau Claire, and in particular, Chancellor James Schmidt, Provost Patricia Kleine, President Kimera Way, Dean David Leaman, Dr. Carmen Manning, Dr. Erica Benson, Dr. Audrey Fessler, Dr. Jenny Shaddock, Dr. Justin Patchin, Dr. Jason Spraitz, Professors Max Garland, Jon Loomis, Allyson Loomis, Molly Patterson, John Hildebrand, and Karen Loeb, as well as Joanne Erickson and Vickie Schafer. I could go on.

Thanks also to my gifted graduate assistants, Alex Long, Laura Becherer, and Josh Bauer—all of whom dug deep to make this a better book—and to my undergraduate students, who make me a better writer through their own work.

In addition, thank you to Dr. Karen Havholm and the Office of Research and Sponsored Programs at the University of Wisconsin–Eau Claire, whose University Research and Creative Activity grant proved vital to this project.

And, lest I forget, the Bama gang, especially those I met on the UAEDFL gridiron.

Thanks, too, to Brendan Todt, for the edits and the correspondence, and to Jill Talbot, for the feedback that eased the doubt.

To Mom, Dad, and brother—can we consider this your Christmas present?

And to my own family, who served as witnesses to my head-pounding, hand-wringing, and tiger-pacing as I tried to tease these essays out.

Finally, thanks to all the nameless folks who didn't just write their way out of disasters, but clawed their way out; the people who did what had to be done *when* it had to be done because they knew no one else was doing it.

THIS IS ONLY A TEST

We can't stop tornadoes. But we can live through them when we know how.

Tornado Warning: A Booklet for Boys and Girls (1981)

I.
DIZZIED

Goodbye, Tuscaloosa

BEFORE

Let me tell you about my wife and my dog and our bathtub. How just minutes prior to the storm—minutes prior to peeling the cushions from the couch and positioning them over our heads—my dog and I stood barefoot in the grass staring up at a swirling sky.

She began to bark at it.

"Quiet," I hissed. "No barking at tornadoes."

I pulled the dog back inside, checked the television, but it wasn't until the power cut out that we were prompted to enter the tub. The meteorologist—who would become a god that day—had just switched from radar screen to video feed, and in those final seconds before we were plunged into darkness, the TV revealed a single gray cloud narrowing as if sucked toward the ground through a straw.

Flashback to the tornado drills of my youth—folded face-to-butt in the bowels of Lindley Elementary in Fort Wayne, Indiana. Face down and neck covered, in the rare moments when the drills turned real, I'd steal a glance at our lion mascot painted on the school's cinderblock walls, hoping he might protect us.

Just days before, during a pep rally, our principal had made one thing clear: "Nobody messes with the Lions!"

Not even tornadoes? I wondered.

Back in the tub now, and there are no lions anywhere, just a dog that for the first time in her life is subdued. We are all humbled that day, but she is the first, her quivering head tucked tightly beneath my knee.

Here, in the bathtub, our privacy is on display: my dandruff shampoo, my wife's pink disposable razor. To the left of these things sits our mango mandarin body wash, which I wonder if we'll ever use again.

My wife's voice overpowers this wondering, overpowers the sound of the tree limbs scraping the bathroom window as well.

"I had to interview a Vietnam vet once," she says from her place beneath a couch cushion. "Back in high school. For social studies. I drove all the way out to his house, and it was when we were having all those really big storms, remember? And so I got there and he said he'd forgotten I was coming. He said his son's home had just gotten blown away and our meeting had slipped his mind."

She'd never found the proper time to tell me this story, but that late afternoon, trapped in a tub, I've at last become a perfect audience.

"We rode around in his golf cart," she continues. "He told me of the destruction he'd seen."

My wife, dog, and I pull closer into our bunker, awaiting what will later be called the second most deadly weather outbreak in recorded history.

Yet somehow, through some luck, we are the glass eye in the storm that sees nothing. And we are the deaf ear, too, hearing only the *drip, drip, drip* of the rusted showerhead.

A moment passes. Then another.

"Is it over yet?" my wife asks, peeking beneath her cushion.

I'm not sure it's even begun.

AFTER

I will spare you the destruction.

You can imagine, I'm sure, what a tree looks like ~~horizontal~~, or a house ~~turned inside out~~. You can imagine also what it means when people say "~~leveled~~." What it means when they say "~~vanished~~."

Stories of ~~legs in~~ the front yard, of ~~victims~~ wrapped in trees ~~like tangled kites~~. Stories of how all that people have left ~~in the world~~ now fits neatly in a grocery cart.

Do not read this too closely. I am trying to spare you ~~the broken glass and the blood.~~

What I can't spare you is the strangeness of living in a tornado-torn town amid writers who, much like myself, have a tendency to turn everything poetic.

Thirteen Ways of Looking at a Black[cloud].

In the [Emergency] Waiting Room

Our poet hands are softer than cream cheese, and though we hardly know how to swing an axe, this doesn't keep us from trying. But eventually we grow tired, sore, and return to our more familiar tools—paper and pen—as we rebuild our town word by word.

But before all that—before the axes and the paper and the pen—my wife, dog, and I wake early to retrace the tornado's path. It's the morning after, and with each step, we try to make sense of our shifted landscape.

But the cars used to be here, I think, running my eyes the length of the empty lot, *so why are they now there?*

Along the route I pick up a newspaper and listen for the prosody in the reports.

Read the repetition: "~~unrelenting~~," "~~unprecedented~~," "~~devastating~~."

And hear the cadence in the quotes: "~~digging with their hands~~," "~~sifted through the remains~~," "~~First responders didn't attend to the dead . . .~~"

Every headline displays the word ~~RAVAGED~~ or ~~RUBBLE~~, and regardless of which story you read, you're told to turn to page 7A.

But not before making a choice:

~~SEE DEATH~~

or

SEE SURVIVORS

The morning after, we see a bit of both.

We join the city's pilgrimage, shuffling directionless down the center lane of 15th Avenue as the sun begins to rise. We are a tailgate without a football game, a processional without a funeral. Through it all, my dog pulls hard on her leash. She doesn't like the sound of ~~chainsaws or shouting or~~ silence, and she is overwhelmed with far too much to sniff—the bolt of cloth flung a hundred yards from Hobby Lobby, the milk bottles still upright in the shell of a Krispy Kreme.

All of this seems like a dream, which is the closest we've come to dreaming in twenty-four hours. We hadn't slept well the previous night, mostly due to the students partying in the apartments behind our house. They'd blared their music louder than the warning sirens, allowing every sound to float down from their balconies, infiltrating our half sleep with shouts for Ping-Pong balls and Solo cups.

But we were kept awake also by the whispers we repeated beneath the sheets—"If we'd died," my wife said, staring at the plus sign on her pregnancy test, "then no one would've known about you."

So many lost so much that day, but we still kept our secret.

A Test of the Emergency Alert System

Directions:

To the best of your ability, please answer the following questions.

1.) Which of the following is not currently found in my bathtub?
   a.) My wife
   b.) My dog
   c.) My unborn child
   d.) Tornado

2.) Which of the following activities are best performed while enduring a disaster in your bathtub?
   a.) Secret sharing
   b.) Secret keeping
   c.) Dog petting
   d.) Scrubbing the tub
   e.) All of the above

3.) Which of the following is the proper response in the immediate aftermath of a disaster?

  a.) Calling family
  b.) Calling friends
  c.) Waiting for the cell phone signal
  d.) Continuing to wait for the cell phone signal
  e.) Leashing your dog
  f.) Unleashing your dog
  g.) Introducing yourself to God
  h.) Introducing God to your wife and dog and unborn child
  i.) Living up to your part of the bargain
  j.) Exiting your house
  k.) Wondering how your plant didn't tip
  l.) Drinking a beer
  m.) Drinking two beers
  n.) Drinking zero beers and remembering your part of the bargain
  o.) Drinking four beers and remembering your part of the bargain
  p.) Pouring your beer in the sink
  q.) In the grass
  r.) In the plant that didn't tip
  s.) Telling your wife the words that got stuck in your throat in that bathtub
  t.) Writing your wife a note—it'll last longer
  u.) Taking a photo—it'll last longer
  v.) Crumbling that note, that photo, and cracking that beer instead
  w.) Unleashing yourself to God
  x.) All of the above

y.) Some of the above

z.) None

4.) True or False: You were just a little scared.

5.) Which of the following newspaper quotations
has been fabricated?

    a.) "We saw it spinning across the street . . ."

    b.) "I was standing at the door and saw it coming."

    c.) ". . . I looked out the window and saw it hovering
       over the lake . . ."

    d.) "I was just trying to get my grandkids something to eat."

    e.) "It just sat there too. Like it was chilling."

    f.) "I have a shell of a home; just four walls."

    g.) "I pulled two dead bodies from a . . ."

    h.) "I found an elderly lady and a three-year-old . . ."

    i.) "People laid blankets over the bodies of neighbors . . ."

    j.) "First responders didn't attend to the dead."

    k.) "It happened too fast to be scared."

    l.) "This just can't be true."

    m.) None

6.) Which of the following tools most effectively removes debris?

    a.) Chainsaw

    b.) Axe

    c.) Bow saw

    d.) Poem

7.) Where is the silver lining?

8.) In what ways did your students respond to your
attempts to contact them?

    a.) With kind assurances of his safety

b.) With concern for your safety

c.) By writing you a poem

d.) By writing you an email

e.) By asking you for her final grade

f.) By thanking you for an "awesome" semester

g.) By wishing you the best of luck in your new job

h.) By wishing you no ill will (despite the B–)

i.) By apologizing for the late paper—"The tornado ate it."

j.) By asking for extra credit

k.) By asking "pretty please" for extra credit

l.) By asking you for your story

m.) By asking you what she's supposed to do now

n.) By asking you "Where is the silver lining?"

o.) By asking you if he'll seriously never see you again

p.) By telling you she'll Facebook you

q.) By telling you that composition class taught him little of survival

r.) By telling you that African American literature taught him little of survival

s.) By writing "The nightmares won't quit coming, will they?"

t.) By writing "TTYL"

u.) By writing

v.) By not writing

w.) With silence

x.) All of the above

y.) Some of the above

z.) None

9.) In the space below, please draw a picture of anything but this.

Essay:

In the space below, please write whatever you must. You can understand, I'm sure, the necessity of writing, even in the dark. Of re-inhabiting a space you'd just as soon forget. I'm asking you not to forget. I'm asking you to remember. To recall the relief you felt in waking up the morning after. And the frustration you felt while mummy-wrapped in the sweat-soaked sheets. Please take a moment to remember the way your foot crunched the cockroach on your walk to the bathroom that night.

Consider the loss of life and all you didn't lose. All you had to lose. All you might've lost had the wind recalculated its route.

Consider infrastructure, pregnancy tests.

Reconsider question #4.

Please, I'm begging you; do not provide specific examples in the space provided below.

_____

_____

_____

_____

_____

_____

Epistle to an Embryo

May 8, 2011

Dear Future Child,

I write to you today so that you might have some account of our first disaster endured as a family. You see, you were there, too, as the tornado swirled overhead.

This is the part of the story we don't tell people because you are not here yet—just some tiny embryo—and the world is too unstable. There are still far too many factors left unaccounted for, too many variables.

Only sometimes, I'm told, does X + Y = BABY.

This morning, while cruising the cereal aisle in the grocery store, your mother nearly gave our secret away. There she was, mulling over the mini-wheats, when confronted by a cereal stocker named Al.

17

"Happy Mother's Day," he told her.

"Thank you."

"*Are* you a mother?" Al inquired, and after a moment's hesitation—after weighing the unforeseen consequences of confiding in a stranger—your mother whispered, "No, but maybe one day."

Al nodded, returning his attention to the toasted oats and filing away the only clue we've yet to offer of your existence.

Now, I admit, Future Child, I know as much of growing babies as Al does. However, in the past few days, I've become accustomed to a new vocabulary—"fallopian," "ovum," "folic acid"—a great flurry of words now left fluttering around our unscathed house.

This is your father's attempt at using his new vocabulary in a sentence:

HOW MANY PLACENTAS DOES IT TAKE TO SCREW IN A LIGHTBULB?

And:

IS IT TIME TO CHANGE THE AMNIOTIC FLUID YET?

I am a poor student, though at least I know the one word we are never to say: ~~miscarry~~, which to me sounds suspiciously like a football snafu, some ill-fated effort in which the ball was not properly tucked in the crook of one's arm.

Let me try another sentence:

I HOPE THAT WE DON'T ~~MISCARRY~~.

You're probably wondering, Future Child, what might lead one to ~~miscarry~~. Is it dependent on the stress of the mother, the split of the cells, the tornado overhead?

All of these things, likely.

I wonder if you could feel our heat as we gathered tight around you. If you had an inkling of what we were learning for the very first time—that your protection suddenly seemed far more important than ours.

And trust me, Bucko, in your current state as an unstable embryo, protecting you is no easy feat. Just imagine holding tight to a poppy seed while on a roller coaster. You are as precarious as the water droplet clinging to our rusted showerhead, as uncertain as the small-clawed squirrel teetering atop the wire outside our house. You are the siren, the silence, the funnel and the cloud. But this is just the start of who you are.

While huddled in our bathtub, I thought, *You are an I, or an almost I,* and was reminded of a poem I taught last spring to a class that hardly cared.

Of the many ways I think of you, I most enjoy imagining you as the almost I; not yet a "he" or a "she" but an "almost." And maybe, if we are lucky, a "soon-to-be." A "person-in-progress." A bucko. *My* bucko. One whose future will be determined by weather and coin flip and fate.

What, I wonder, will the universe decide for you?

Which you will you be?

Will you buy the corsage or the boutonniere?

Which talks shall I reserve for your mother?

Though perhaps since your conception occurred so close to the tornado's birth, you will come out half tornado, instead; a cross-pollination of sorts, your abnormality invisible on one Doppler screen, but wholly visible on another.

Let's pretend, for argument's sake, that you do leave the womb spinning. What are we to do with you then? How do we swaddle your swirling shape? How do we confine you to a crib?

Fatherhood, I'm told, is hard enough without the convergence of cumulonimbus and vapor, though perhaps this is the unique challenge with which we've been blessed. Our penance for survival.

And let's not even discuss your adolescence where, just for spite, when I say "Don't you even think about blowing down the neighbor's mailbox!" you'll blow down his gazebo instead.

Or his tree. Or all of our trees.

Have I told you about the time your mother and I dreamed up an alternative ending to our lives? How from our place beneath that rusted showerhead, we whispered prophecies?

If we die here nobody will ever know about . . .

We barely even knew of you ourselves. Just three days removed from the plus sign on the pregnancy test, the new world stretched before us still seemed unfathomable.

We could not conceive that we had conceived.

What universe, we wondered, would allow for such a thing?

But as our house creaked and our neighborhood swayed, what suddenly seemed most unfathomable was our lives stripped of that future. We'd interpreted the plus sign as a promise, and we expected the universe to make good.

But the universe provided us far fewer tea leaves than oak leaves, and predicting our future on how foliage fell seemed suddenly less than ideal.

Outside that bathroom window, an oak tree as old as the Civil War stretched its limbs and bowed down to us.

As I imagined its roots uprooting, I thought of the old koan:

If a tree falls in the forest and nobody is there to hear it, does it make a sound?

It must.

Because what is the alternative? That we believe only that which we can see and hear and feel? That there is no place in the world for an almost I?

Trust me, Bucko, when a tree falls it makes a terrible sound.

Swear to me you didn't hear it.

To the Good People of Joplin

May 23, 2011

To the Good People of Joplin:

This will get worse before it gets better. I know this because of what I've observed from my own firsthand experiences in Tuscaloosa, a city much like yours which was ravaged a month prior to your own ravaging. Likely you watched us from afar, which is what we do now, our cities forever wedded by our season of misfortune.

Allow me to share with you a difficult truth:

In the coming hours and days your death count is likely to rise. Cell phone reception will return—which, on the surface, seems like a good thing, though this increased communication will mostly only bring bad news. People will begin to learn who was lost and how, and as their stories are sifted from the rubble, it will soon become clear that everybody knows somebody now gone. You will begin hearing stories, though unlike the phone calls not all of them will end badly. Like the one where the bathtub blows away but the family remains safely inside; and the one where the dog survives two weeks on broken legs before reuniting with his people.

In short, take comfort where you can.

As the dust settles, people will begin endowing the storm with a conscience. They will talk about how the tornado leveled one house but left another, how it *made that choice*. You will begin fitting nature's lunacy into some strange logic, bring God into the equation and speak of "master plans" not yet revealed to his flock. This is a good technique, and one that we have found to be quite useful here in Tuscaloosa. The fitting together of disjoint pieces offers the same distraction as any good puzzle—an outlet to busy oneself when the mind is in need of rest.

I should warn you, though, that you'll soon be inundated by a storm of another sort.

Everyone will want to help you, and even those of you who were spared the worst of it will receive a knock on your door, someone pleading with you to take a bottle of water.

Listen to me: just take it. This is a small gift from a person who feels as helpless as you do. Better still if you can muster a stoic smile, though you'll surely be forgiven if you can't.

Good people of Joplin, I can't promise you much, but I can promise you this: one month from today, you will not be healed, but you will be healing.

The scrap will be piled alongside the roads, and eventually even the choir of sirens will dissipate. One day soon, cars will once again outnumber ambulances, and in a few weeks' time, you'll see a child fling a Frisbee and forget that anything more treacherous ever circled in the wind.

This morning, as my cereal turned soggy, I watched the on-site meteorologist from the Weather Channel choke up on the air. He was describing your world turned inside out, your people stumbling, when he momentarily misplaced his own stoic smile and admitted that Joplin looked "very reminiscent of what we saw last month in [pause] Tuscaloosa."

His pause said what his words couldn't, reminding me of one final piece of advice that I'll bestow upon you now.

You will find, I think, that the inexplicable nature of nature is another hard-earned side effect of your troubles. And more to the point, that seeking answers in the aftermath is a Sisyphean task not worth your effort.

For a month now, I have been trying to write my way out of disaster.

It is still here.

Fifty Ways of Looking at Tornadoes

1.

For nine months now, I have been trying to write my way out of disaster. I thought it would be easier than this. Yet no matter how many times I report on that April afternoon in Tuscaloosa—when my wife, dog, and I hid in our bathtub—still, the storm will not leave us.

2.

Once I made them by hand. You can make one, too. Pour a teaspoon of salt into a cylindrical glass and spin the spoon clockwise. Or counterclockwise. It doesn't matter.

3.

I am not the first to have fashioned one. In 1955, New York University's James E. Miller placed a pan of water in a circular box, positioning air slits on either side. The water was heated, emitting steam, and as additional air blew in, that steam grew into a cyclone.

4.

Do not be fooled by the aforementioned examples of scientific ingenuity: humankind did not invent the tornado, nor has it improved upon the design.

5.

Prior to creating them, we created warning systems against them. In October of 1883, Edward S. Holden issued a call for an "apparatus" that might provide towns a few minutes' warning before a tornado's impending touchdown. He suggested a highly elaborate network of bells, even created a prototype—a wired bell that rang upon exposure to a particular velocity of wind. Perhaps inspired by the recent invention of Alexander Graham Bell's telephone, Holden envisioned spools of underground wires connecting house to house and person to person, ensuring safety for all.

6.

Despite Holden's dreams of connectivity, findings from a 1972 study by professors John Sims and Duane Baumann noted a division instead: "The number of tornado-caused deaths in the South is strikingly higher than it is in the remainder of the nation." Sims and Baumann argued that this regional discrepancy was due, in part, to variations in housing structure, though also to philosophical differences on the subject of danger. According to the report, while in the midst of a tornado watch, 24.2 percent of Illinoisans kept an eye tilted to the television, while 0.0 percent of Alabamians reacted in kind. Instead, Sims and Baumann explained, Alabamians much preferred "the method of using one's own senses—they 'watch the sky' or 'look at the clouds.'" It was a strategy deemed "psychologically anachronistic," a behavior from a bygone era in which the tomfoolery of front-porch reconnaissance somehow overpowered the precision of science. Illinoisans relied on radar for up-to-the-minute weather reports, while seven hundred miles to the south Alabamians preferred confronting "the whirlwind alone with [their] God."

7.

It is a comfort, perhaps, for southerners to look their maker in the eye, though when I—a northern transplant—rode out Tuscaloosa's storm, I looked to no one. Looked *at* no one, either. I was not alone in that bathtub (I had my wife, our dog, our unborn child), but we with eyes aimed them low, tucking our heads tight beneath the couch cushions.

8.

Thirty years prior, in April of 1981, the Department of Commerce released a public service announcement entitled *Tornado Warning: A Booklet for Boys and Girls.* Featuring the lovable Owlie Skywarn—an owl with a penchant for tornado spotting—the feathered fowl took children on a guided tour of the necessary facts for surviving a tornado. "Keep track of sunshine," Skywarn hoots. "Your town needs you."

9.

Towns need survivors to survive.

10.

I thought I was paying a price just by surviving. Thought that if I wrote enough, paid my portion of the tribute, it might just blow away from us for good. It hasn't. We tried leaving it instead, packing our bags and relocating 1,012 miles to the north. Still, it sleeps beside me on the pillow. This very moment, I can hear it rattling around in the vents.

11.

Alabama has a long history of leveling, though few remember what occurred in Tuscumbia, Alabama, at dinnertime on November 22, 1874. How ten were killed, thirty injured, and half the town rattled to rubble. Or what occurred in Leeds, Alabama, a decade later, on February 19, at 1:20 in the afternoon: eleven dead, thirty-one injured, "hail of unusual size . . ."

12.

Let's jump ahead now to March 21, 1932, when again tornadoes tore through the state. Within forty-eight hours, Alabama reported 200 dead, though the number soon climbed to 268. In the days that followed, the stories, like the body count, began to grow. One recounted how three-year-old Douglas Sims was flung into a field after being ripped from his father's arms. As Douglas's parents began their frantic search to retrieve him, one newspaper reported, lightning "revealed the youngster nearly 50 feet away walking towards them with outstretched arms."

13.

They say that lightning never strikes twice, but this does not hold true for tornadoes. Ask the people of Irving, Kansas, who on May 30, 1879, endured a pair of tornadoes less than an hour apart.

On May 4, 1922, Austin, Texas, too, received a one-two tornadic punch. Though perhaps the dubious honor of most regularly struck town goes to Codell, Kansas, a place that received not two tornadoes in close succession, but three, each just one year apart. May 20, 1916, was a bad day for the people of Codell, but so was May 20 the year after, and May 20 the year after that.

14.

Ask meteorologists, they'll tell you: Tornadoes keep careful calendars.

15.

Meteorologists will also tell you that tornadoes share a lexicon with humans. Tornadoes, much like their victims, are born, die, and live a life in between. They travel in "families" (formed from "parent storms"), and are known to chase one another as if they were the "It" in a game of backyard tag.

16.

On April 27, 2011, the "It" tagged Tuscaloosa.

17.

"You can't stop a tornado," hoots Skywarn. "You can't keep it from hitting a house or town . . . But people can get out of its way."

18.

On April 11, 1965, the people of Toledo tried just that. It struck anyhow, bringing with it something strange. The strangeness came in the form of two streams of parallel light, along with a cloud filled with lightning bolts "shooting straight ahead like arrows." The tornado was said to be encircled by an "electric blue light," as well as by "balls of orange and lightning" trailing from the tip of the tail. Do not expect science to explain any of this. One witness added that the tornado's tail was reminiscent of an elephant trunk. "It would dip down as if to get food," the witnesses described, "then rise up again . . . [to] put the food in his mouth."

19.

When tornadoes are hungry, they will eat a Krispy Kreme—not the donut, but the shop. The storm devoured the building's shell, but the ice cooler remained intact. And an even greater mystery: each bottle of milk remained upright.

20.

Tornadoes, once, were a mystery. As a result of the devastation wrought by the East Baltic tornado of June 22, 1795, Johann Christoph Brotze—a teacher and historian from present-day Latvia—created a sketch of a sketch of a tornado. He had not witnessed it himself, though he based his work on a curious drawing he'd seen. Brotze's sketch, believed to be one of our earliest depictions of a tornado, revealed mostly what was expected—a cone-shaped cloud narrowing to a tail just beneath a blanket of darkness. Brotze's tornado showed no swirling motion, but instead appeared to be holding firm, a god's muscled torso surrounded by lightning bolts, his head hidden just out of frame.

21.

Tornadoes, twice, were a mystery. John Parker Finley, an accomplished Army Signal Service officer, dedicated much of his life trying to understand them. Most nineteenth-century Americans had never seen a real one, but with his 1887 illustrated book on the subject, Finley brought tornadoes into American households everywhere.

22.

Tornadoes, thrice, were a mystery. A 1967 article in *Science News* admitted that while "hundreds of tornadoes maul the surface of the earth every year, taking hundreds of lives and smashing all but the sturdiest of man's works . . . they remain one of the least understood of natural phenomena."

23.

Perhaps our lack of understanding isn't due to the scientific uncertainty of the phenomena, but our inability to fit tornadoes into a moral framework. When nature kills, we find excuses for its behavior. When a mountain climber dies, a part of us faults the climber for traversing such treacherous terrain. Likewise, when a sailor drowns, we wonder what business that sailor had in the sea in the first place. *Couldn't you see Death,* we think, *just lurking beneath those shadowy waves?*

24.

I swear to you, we took no chances in Tuscaloosa. We climbed no peaks, swam no seas—nobody tempted anyone. Earlier that afternoon, my wife and I humbly sat across from one another at an Indian buffet on 15th Street. A few hours later, that restaurant became a demarcation line.

25.

Eight days later, I drove down what remained of 15th Street and was surprised to find Central High School's football team already packed back into their practice pads. The school had been spared by half a mile. I remember thinking: *Look at those boys hustling to make the tackle.* And then: *Hustling to evade more than tackles.*

26.

Tornadoes bruise, too, though sometimes they destroy places rather than people—an unintentional mercy. They have been known to force the caps off jam jars and strip the bark from trees, the feathers from chickens. I try to imagine it: a flash of lightning, followed by the image of a chicken recklessly plucked, goose-bumped and shivering on the edge of an empty field.

27.

On the final page of *Tornado Warning*, the still-feathered Owlie Skywarn is pictured with his wings wrapped around a pair of smiling children. "We can't stop tornadoes," Skywarn chides. "But we can live through them when we know how."

28.

Trust me when I tell you that on April 27, 2011, Owlie Skywarn didn't give one hoot for Tuscaloosa.

29.

I am struggling to put this into perspective.

30.

(I am still struggling to put this into perspective.)

31.

In 1884, James Macfarlane, too, struggled with perspective. He had observed many tears in the land, believing them the handi-work of unrecorded tornadoes. "There is evidence in the forests of Pennsylvania that many localities have been visited by tor-nadoes of which no accounts have ever been recorded," he ex-plained, noting that sometimes the damage was concentrated in a small region rather than along the typical swaths cut through the trees. According to Macfarlane, the once carefully combed earth appeared oddly uprooted—evidence of an edited country. Why were there no warnings?

32.

The morning prior to the tornado, the front page of *The Tuscaloosa News* gave us our warning. One article began: "Here we go again." Throughout much of the spring, storms had struck regularly, perhaps causing some Tuscaloosans to downplay the seriousness of the situation.

33.

Survivors are always survivors until they aren't.

34.

Fresh off the success of his previous work, Owlie Skywarn returned a few years later, this time in coloring-book form. "Listen for the tornado's roar," says Skywarn. "Some people say it sounds like a thousand trains."

35.

Others, like me, heard nothing but the showerhead's *drip, drip, drip* . . .

36.

In the rec center locker room later that week, I overheard the old men convene their morning meeting. First item on the agenda: discussing the latest body unearthed—a friend of a friend of a friend. "I've never been afraid of anything in my life," explained one. "But next time I hear the wind moving like that, I know I'll be heading for cover."

Define "cover."

By Friday, April 29, we were still without power, but that is all we were without. We still had our lives, our dog, our unborn child. This is the definition of privilege.

In a 1935 edition of *Transactions of the Kansas Academy of Science,* John Copley wrote, "It has been my privilege to observe several tornadoes at close range and also to examine the effects of others."

(Please see #38 for a true definition of "privilege.")

"For people getting their animals back, we usually make them show ID, but a lot of them just don't have it; they don't have anything," an animal shelter representative explained to *The Tuscaloosa News.* "So we're going on gut instincts and the reaction of the animal."

Hours prior to landing on Tuscaloosa's airstrip, President Obama trusted his gut and ordered Seal Team Six to move. Then he turned to our town, walked our rubble, whispered, "I've never seen destruction like this."

On Monday, May 2, *The Tuscaloosa News* likely became the only newspaper in America in which the death of Osama bin Laden was not the lead.

44.

There is a calculus to measuring destruction.

45.

But there is no calculus to a cumulonimbus.

46.

No equation to measure the rattling coming from deep inside my vents.

47.

All we know for sure is that tornadoes, like essays, demand the proper conditions.

48.

But do not ask what those conditions are.

49.

Because tornadoes, always, are a mystery.

50.

And essays, like bathtubs, provide only temporary relief.

The Longest Wait

We have been waiting for you for nine months now, but still you are not here. On the longest days, I make a beeping sound, then turn to my phone, tell your mother, "Hey, I got a text. Says sorry it's late, but it'll be here any minute."

You're not.

You are not here one minute and you are not here the next.

Are we concerned by your late arrival? Yes, secretly, though the midwives insist that your tardiness is hardly unusual.

Relax. Babies do not wear wristwatches.

This seems like sound advice.

Nevertheless, TV has convinced us that there must be scientific certainty to your arrival.

We understand that there is to be the breaking of water, the white-knuckled pushing, and then you are ours—promptly at forty weeks.

Better late than never, I tell your mother, and when that doesn't work, I say, *Hey, at least it's not an if, but a when.*

We are grateful that you are a when, and we are equally grateful that you held tight when that tornado tore through our town. You were just a poppy seed then, half a thumbnail bobbing in an endless ocean, the definition of vulnerable.

Your mother, the dog, and I were vulnerable too, taking refuge in a bathroom in a duplex in a cul-de-sac at the edge of a road at a corner of a street in a city that nearly blew away.

We'll tell you all about it when you're older, but it will be hard for you to understand. How the wind picked up, and then picked up everything with it. How the meteorologist shouted "Safe place!" before fading from the screen.

A friend says, *Take long walks!* so we climb the mountain-sized hill behind our house.

We are half a country away from that bathtub now, from that storm, and so we wear boots—not flip-flops—as we slog through Wisconsin's snow.

Alabama has become an afterthought, though it is also a before-thought, and a during-thought, and a constant thought.

Most days I try to forget but I always just remember.

From atop the mountain-sized hill behind our house, the wind blows colder, cutting into your mother's face. Yet she—so determined to sweat you out—hardly seems to notice. Your future dog, too, points her nose uphill, completing our weatherworn trio.

One day, I think, *you will make us a quartet,* but that day is not today.

Sometimes, after our walks, I listen as your mother pounds up and down stairs bargaining with God.

I will walk these a thousand times if you will release it. We have been waiting for so long now. Please, try to understand.

But we are not surprised when you do not come that day. Or the day after.

After all, we've tried bargaining with God before, praying for strong foundations, for reinforced walls, for trajectories that do not lead to us.

On Monday there are contractions; we both have them. Mine aren't the same as hers, just shaky nerves in the minute prior to kick-off. Alabama is playing LSU for the national championship, so we bundle ourselves in team sweatshirts in solidarity for a place we once called home. The previous fall, we lived so close to Bryant-Denny stadium that our windows rattled with the touchdowns. And then, one afternoon in April there was a touch down of another sort.

The game is scoreless and then it is not: a field goal, followed by another, and another. Suddenly Alabama is up by nine, and while your mother's mild contractions continue, we distract ourselves with football talk. We decide to wait out the pain for a while, feigning focus on the screen.

Our dog senses something is awry. She patters down the stairs and hides beneath our bed—the safest place in the house besides the bathroom.

There is another contraction, followed by another, and we are timing them now, feeling out the space between them.

At the end of the first quarter, your mother calls the hospital: *Hi, I have been having painful contractions . . . fluctuating between three and five minutes . . . baby one, but I'm almost at forty-one weeks*

... hopefully ... not quite yet ... we've just been waiting for so long now ...

They keep us waiting longer.

And so, she collapses onto the couch so we can debate halfbacks and running backs for a few quarters more.

But with six minutes left in the fourth, your mother decides we've waited long enough.

Her contractions have lengthened, quickened, tightened, and while we're both anxious to watch the final minutes (well, me more than her), we are less anxious to birth you in our living room.

We buckle up and drive down Ferry Street, bypassing the Dairy Queen and taking a shortcut through the park. At last, we turn on Whipple Street, parking on the second story of the garage. "Yakety Yak" blares throughout the three-minute drive, which seems appropriate given the lunacy of reproduction.

While we fill out paperwork, Trent Richardson runs for a touchdown. While we settle into our room, Coach Saban hoists the trophy. We, of course, are privy to none of it.

"Turn on the game," your mother suggests as she slips into her hospital gown. We search for it, but the game is now gone, nothing left but infomercials.

Eventually, a sports channel begins replaying the game in its entirety, and as your mother grips my hand, breathes deep, we stare at the screen together.

It feels redundant, watching the plays already played and always knowing the outcome. But we like knowing—a contrast to our current state of knowing nothing at all.

The nurse is kind, and as I doze off in a chair beside the bed, she drapes a warm blanket over my shoulders. The entire room is trapped in half sleep, though when our eyes momentarily bob back to the television screen, we see not a football game, but the footage they've been replaying during each Alabama game all season: the foreboding cloud hovering over the football stadium, the tornado that thumped our town.

"We survived that," I mumble to the nurse.

It's 3:00 AM or later.

"Pardon?"

"We survived . . ."

"Tornado," your mother explains between contractions. "We *survived* that."

We recite our story, but it makes less sense now than ever.

How we crouched in a tub with our poppy seed child and were somehow not blown away.

"It went right by our house," your mother says between contractions. I nod to confirm it, staring once more at the tornado on the screen, and wondering how—nine months later and 1,012 miles away—it still managed to find us.

Your mother is in a different bathtub now, a swollen fish trying to push you out. We are no longer afraid of what's outside our window, but of what's inside her instead.

You, you are what scares us. You and nature both.

The water helps, your mother says, so she rocks back and forth in the tub.

Hours later, when the real work begins, I will begin to better understand devastation. Will see your mother's face buckle like her legs never did on that mountain-sized hill behind our house. There are no trembling lips, just promises to God and curses to God and apologies to God as well. We remember our part of the bargain—*Be grateful!*—and so we are, knowing full well that even an interminable wait is a gift some never receive.

The midwife says push, and your mother pushes.

All I say is "It's coming closer now," though this time we don't take cover.

I tremble as you become you—an I—and your body bursts into cold light.

First you breathe and then you don't but then, dear boy, you do again.

Let us try the strength of these waters
that drowned our friends . . .

—LORD BYRON, as reported in Edward Trelawny's
Recollections of the Last Days of Shelley and Byron (1858)

II.
DROWNED

The Girl in the Surf

You may have heard of these pictures before: the ones of the girl in the surf on Plum Island. At least, I'd always heard the figure was a girl, though when I actually *saw* the photos I came to understand otherwise: she is a woman, and while she is a breathing woman in one frame she has stopped breathing in the next.

The photos were taken by Marc Halevi, a photojournalist on assignment to capture the highest tides to have reached Plum Island, Massachusetts, in over half a century. Instead, he captured the effects of those tides—a woman drowning.

What we know of the woman's last moments we know only from Halevi's photos and witness testimony. The woman was believed to have been drinking that day and, prior to the drowning, reportedly mumbled, "Let the ocean take me." Yet when the water did take her—gripping a beer bottle in one hand, a cigarette in the other—people began wondering if her death was intentional and, more to the point, whether Halevi might have prevented it.

Halevi's photos have become a staple in the media ethics classroom. Is it the photojournalist's obligation to intervene on behalf of a stranger? And, if so, is this form of intervention a moral imperative shared by all? The story is complicated further when we learn that Halevi's seemingly close proximity to the victim is an illusion, the result of a telephoto lens. In reality, he was nearly fifty feet away from the woman, and when he spotted two men (one of whom happened to be a lifeguard) rushing to her aid, he held firm, his finger on the shutter release. While some view Halevi's inaction as opportunistic (if not outright ghoulish), others defend him, arguing that lifesaving was best attempted by a trained lifeguard, and that Halevi's role that day was to perform the function for which *he'd* been trained—to keep the subject always in frame, to shoot until the film ran out.

My camera was out of batteries the day Tuscaloosa was destroyed by an EF4 tornado

In the days that followed, we who survived took to the streets, uncertain of how to act.

We began thinking in terms of what we had and what we could do.

I have an axe, so I must chop this fallen tree.

I have hands, so I must move this rubble.

We embraced our role as witnesses to disaster, carefully surveying what remained of the worst-hit neighborhoods, trying to deduce how words like "velocity" and "trajectory" had transformed whole houses into shells.

One morning a few days after the storm, a friend and I walked through one of the hardest-hit neighborhoods; armed with her camera, we tried capturing some portion of the storm's destruction. We felt it our obligation for the same reason we chopped trees and moved rubble:

I have a camera, so I must take this picture.

Though we had little control over the relief efforts, we knew how to point and click.

First, we snapped photos of a lake filled with debris, of car windows shattered. We snapped a few of the downed power lines, too, their coils curled like black snakes along the tree trunks. Never meant to be souvenirs, these pictures were our humble attempt to do something useful. As writers in grad school, we had been trained to believe that stories mattered, that remembering mattered, and that if we did a good enough job recounting these stories then we might matter, too.

In one instance a police officer asked us to "take it easy" with the pictures, to respect the victims' privacy. We complied. After all, how were we to explain what we'd convinced ourselves were the subtle differences between exploitation and documentation, particularly to someone who had witnessed so much of the former?

Twenty-four hours after the storm, I watched as a carnival atmosphere consumed what was left of our town—people clogging the streets in SUVs, the passengers half-hanging out the windows. Everybody clutched iPhones and video cameras, capturing what little remained. They "oohed" and "ahhed" as if watching a fireworks display, took selfies amid the storm-ravaged topography. They gobbled up gigabytes, uploaded all they could.

Little was salvaged, but everything was saved.

On May 22, less than a month after our experience, Joplin, Missouri, endured its own disaster. An EF5 tornado decimated the town, and as I watched the news footage over breakfast, I was overcome by a sickening déjà vu. Hadn't we seen this one before? Hadn't it already played out?

Feeling mostly helpless, I thought about all that I still had.

I have a pen, so I will write a letter to Joplin.

My letter ran in a few St. Louis newspapers, warning Joplin residents that as a tornado survivor myself, I knew for certain that "this will get worse before it gets better." The letter was well received, and for a week I received phone calls from radio stations and journalists throughout Missouri, asking me for interviews about my experiences in Tuscaloosa. I obliged, always willing to open my mouth, though I hardly knew anything. My own house had been spared, after all, and at the storm's conclusion, when I walked outside to assess the damage, all I found was that there was nothing to assess. We remained wholly intact, right down to the potted plant on the porch.

Yet the people of Joplin had hardly been so lucky, and my letter to its citizens—gloomy content aside—went momentarily viral, enticing Missourians I'd never met to Facebook me, Follow me, and call upon me for answers. Columnists quoted the letter; pastors, too.

"People really love it," one interviewer informed me. "We've gotten all kinds of calls from churches who can't wait to read it at Sunday service."

I was the wrong spokesman, and yet I just kept speaking.

I told them that the death counts would continue to rise, and that when the cell phone reception returned, it would only bring bad news. I was no prophet—just a guy who couldn't shut up—and in an attempt at solidarity, I went so far as to assure the people of Joplin that our towns would be "forever wedded by our shared season of misfortune." But what did I know of misfortune?

Days later, when the letter reached a producer affiliated with Diane Sawyer's *World News*, I was asked for an interview yet again. And yet again, I was happy to comply.

I have a voice, so I must share our story with the world.

The film crew situated me in front of a few leveled houses half a mile from my own upright house. For five excruciating minutes as the camera rolled, I rambled on about "town pride" and "camaraderie" and "communities coming together." I sprinkled in a few uplifting catchphrases as well, working in "but there will be brighter days ahead" more times than I'm comfortable admitting.

In retrospect, my intentions seem obvious. I was a cheerleader for the living—proof that some of us were still okay. Yet I could fulfill this role only when I refrained from looking at the destruction behind me. Eyes forward, chin up, I stared into the camera and assured the nation that Joplin, like Tuscaloosa, would undoubtedly endure.

Diane Sawyer's *World News* never aired the footage. Once again, I had been spared. I had nothing of value to add, and as I turned on the news the following evening, I was relieved to watch B-roll from other people's stories, instead. I received my message loud and clear: People had heard enough from B. J. Hollars.

If the interview had gone longer, I might've described to Diane Sawyer's crew how my wife and I rode out the storm in a bathtub, our only inconvenience a dripping showerhead. I might also have admitted that we watched a romantic comedy that night, burning the battery from her laptop, while just out of earshot, people cried for help.

"*Maybe* your town will recover," I should have explained to the camera. "I guess I really don't know."

Marc Halevi was likely equally uncertain of the outcome from his photos of the woman in the surf. Could hardly have predicted the debate he'd spur from what developed on the beach and in the darkroom. Perhaps writers and photojournalists are alike in that we can only seem to find answers in the aftermath. Yet as reporters of truth, perhaps our first responsibility is simply to tell it, to scribble and to click. When we start down the path of parsing what *portion* of truth we feel obligated to tell—abridged or unabridged—perhaps we do a disservice to our readers and viewers. Simply put, reporters of truth (be it through words or pictures) are bound to a different set of rules than fiction writers and illustrators. We work at a disadvantage because we don't create the stories, nor are we capable of divining their endings. In nonfiction, "happily ever after" is always a possibility but never a guarantee, though this in no way diminishes our need to recount these stories regardless. "The truth is in the telling" (or so the adage goes) and as a writer, it is my job simply to tell it.

At least that's what I thought in the moments before all my self-righteous rules went out the window.

You see, less than forty-eight hours after I completed a draft of this essay, a young man drowned in the river behind my house. As I began my first early morning jog in my new town I noticed a bevy of police officers and rescue personnel peering into the river. To my right, a boy in a still-wet swimsuit leaned over a car's driver's-side window to share news with the girl inside. I overheard what I could while jogging past, though in truth, I didn't hear much.

The story revealed itself later: How the young man and an acquaintance attempted to swim from the nearby island back to shore. How the pair became separated in the dark water. How one made it back but one didn't.

No telephoto lens captured anything.

No lifeguards were called in to assist.

The next morning, my wife, dog, and I walked the riverbank directly across from that island. We were not looking for a body, but we found one—a middle-aged man tromping his way through the brush. I asked him if there had been any updates on the search, to which the man replied that no, they had yet to find his nephew.

"Nephew?" I asked.

For the next ten minutes we spoke with the victim's uncle, and he told us many things that I will not repeat here.

Perhaps a better writer would repeat them, would take my earlier advice and simply "tell it" via scribble and click. But for me, the story—still ongoing—isn't yet ready to be told. Or at least I'm not ready to tell it. There is nothing to save, only something to salvage, and what good can words possibly do?

Let the body first be pulled from the river, I think. *Maybe I'll tell it then.*

Dispatches from
the Drownings

1.

It is our first night in a new town and we sleep soundly. Brush teeth, crawl beneath sheets, and listen to the crickets just beyond the bedroom window. There is a river beyond the window, and in that river, a boy. A boy who—we will learn the next day—has the river inside of him, too.

2.

Our lives begin in the water. In utero, a fetus relies solely on its mother's water-based womb. Oxygen is not yet introduced through the fetal lungs, but through the umbilical cord—a more direct route. Nevertheless, with the snip of the scissors, this route closes for good. *Dear Child, if you wish to live, you must try to trust your lungs . . .*

3.

On the third day, God divided water from earth and two days later he filled them. "Let the waters swarm with swarms of living creatures," he cried, "and let birds fly above the earth in the open firmament of heaven." Despite his miracle, God's work remained incomplete. On the sixth day God created humans, endowing us with lungs and free will. Sixteen hundred years later, he drowned us like dogs in the Flood.

4.

As the nineteenth century turned into the twentieth, thirty-eight dogs were drowned in the name of science. Professor E. A. Schafer of the Royal Medical and Chirurgical Society held them beneath the water to gain insight into how life leaves a body.

5.

Holocaust (n.): destruction or slaughter on a mass scale, esp. caused by fire . . .

6.

Since God chose water, do we call it a mass execution instead?

7.

French royalists were no strangers to mass executions. In 1793–1794, those loyal to the crown were often condemned to death by drowning. By year's end, revolutionary Jean-Baptiste Carrier had water on his hands. In the city of Nantes, he ordered the drowning of an estimated four thousand royalists in the Loire River. Carrier dubbed the Loire the "National Bathtub"—a nod to the guillotine, which was dubbed the "National Razor."

8.

Others, too, had water on their minds. When man could not decide if a witch was a witch, the witch was hurled into the river. The tests were always conclusive: the innocent sank while the guilty stayed afloat.

9.

In Archimedes's book, *On Floating Bodies* (250 BCE), the founder of hydrostatics notes, "Any body wholly or partially immersed in a fluid experiences an upward force equal to the weight of the fluid displaced." Translation: Anybody smaller than the body of water in which the body is placed is capable of floating. Translation: Adherence to the principles of science may be an admission of witchcraft.

10.

By the eighteenth century, drowning victims were not treated with hands clasped in prayer, but hands clasped to a chest. Though resuscitation seemed like witchcraft, God himself had given us the clues. In Genesis, he breathed life into Adam's nostrils, and humans took careful note.

11.

On December 14, 1650, Anne Greene—sentenced for murdering her stillborn child—was hanged in Oxford, England. She refused to die. Greene's friends tugged on her dangling legs to hasten Death, but Death refused to be hurried. When at last it was believed that Death had taken mercy on her, Greene's body was placed in a coffin. But even there she retained a spark of life. In an attempt to extinguish it, a merciful man struck her hard on the chest, but the blow only served to further restore her. Let the record show that they could not kill Anne Greene, despite their best efforts. However, this incident was not viewed as the world's first successful resuscitation attempt, but as a miracle. It was God's hand—not the merciful man's—that was credited with saving her life.

12.

Yet men wanted credit as well. In 1767, citizens and physicians in Amsterdam created the Dutch Society to Rescue People from Drowning. Their mission: to promote resuscitation in drowning victims. Their primary promotion involved awarding medals to those who saved a life. The medals depicted a cloaked woman with a hand clutching a drowned man. Yet it is the cloaked woman's other hand that matters, the one that halted the scythe-wielding Death like a stubborn crossing guard.

13.

On November 16, 1793, the crossing guard was nowhere. And so Jean-Baptiste Carrier shoved ninety priests into the National Bathtub. Death gorged on eighty-seven of them, but nowhere in his expanding waistline could he find room for the remaining three. Miraculously, the three priests floated downriver and were rescued by a warship. The ship's captain provided the priests with drink and blankets; they had been brought back to life. The following day, the priests were returned to Jean-Baptiste Carrier; they had been brought back to Death.

14.

A year old now, my son knows that when the conditions are right, bath time can be fun. These conditions include warm water, "No Tears" shampoo, and his trusty rubber duck. Other conditions:

It is not November 1793. Jean-Baptiste Carrier is nowhere to be found.

15.

On July 8, 1822, Percy Bysshe Shelley and a pair of Englishmen set sail from Leghorn to Lerici in the schooner *Don Juan*. Prior to boarding, Shelley supposedly spotted his doppelgänger warning him against the trip. Shelley ignored him and drowned. How are we to interpret such an act? As a premonition? As prophecy? Or as some mythmaker's attempt to allow Shelley to perish poetically?

16.

Josef Mengele—also known as the Angel of Death—allowed no one to perish poetically. The Nazi doctor who'd busied himself tearing hearts from Jewish bodies found one day that he could not control his own. It beat for the last time while he was out for a swim off the coast of Brazil in February of 1979.

17.

Who are the victims of drownings? They are not all Nazi war criminals. According to the most recent data from the Centers for Disease Control and Prevention, they are mostly males and minorities. "The fatal drowning rate of African American children ages 5–14 is almost three times that of white children in the same age range," the CDC notes.

18.

These statistics prove particularly true if you are a fourteen-year-old black boy named Emmett Till in 1955. He was drowned in the Tallahatchie River—though only after he was beaten and shot and weighed down in the water by a cotton gin fan barbwired around his neck.

19.

I'm elbow-deep in my soapy sink when my wife says, "Thanks for doing the dishes." When I don't respond, she reminds me that she prepared dinner, that this is our arrangement. "I know," I say. "I'm not complaining." She says I look grumpy, and I tell her I'm not even thinking about the dishes. "Are you thinking about drowning?" she asks. "Of course not," I say, but what I'm thinking is *I'm always thinking about drowning.*

20.

When we speak of the river, we often speak of it in human terms. The river is rough. Dangerous. Unforgiving. The river is brutal and cruel. Emmett Till's murderers were also all of these things, as well as innocent—at least according to the all-white, all-male jury in that Mississippi courtroom in 1955.

21.

You know this story by now. How I was out for a jog in July when I spotted the police car pulled to the side of the road alongside the river. How I observed the people gesticulating toward the water, and since I was curious—not to mention breathless—I used the distraction as an excuse to momentarily rest. I paused just long enough to overhear an officer say that the boy was believed to have drowned. That was the moment I picked up my pace. The moment I learned I knew nothing of breathlessness.

22.

Shelley's body was burned beachside in August of 1822. Overseeing his departure were his friends: Lord Byron, Edward Trelawny, and Leigh Hunt. But Shelley's boatman, Edward Williams, was the first to burn. As he did, a grief-stricken Byron turned his attention to the sea. "Let us try the strength of these waters that drowned our friends," Byron challenged as he charged into the water. After a few strokes he was driven back by cramps.

23.

We can only speculate what masterworks Shelley might have written had he heeded the advice of his doppelgänger. Or at least the advice offered in a 2012 article from the Centers for Disease Control and Prevention: "Learn to swim."

24.

In 1892, I. D. Johnson's *A Guide to Homeopathic Practice* provided information on how best to save a drowning victim. "Now, with one hand upon the back and the other upon the abdomen, press gently for about two seconds," Johnson explained; "then turn the body well upon the face, and repeat the pressing as before; in this way strive to induce artificial respiration by the alternate pressure upon the abdomen and rotation of the body."

25.

When I think of putting pressure on a body, I think of Josef Mengele.

26.

But let us not overlook the Romans. How in Rome, if a man was found guilty of murdering a family member, he could be sewn into a sack with any number of live animals—cock, viper, ape—and hurled into the unforgiving water.

27.

Which begs the question: How many apes were available for drowning in ancient Rome?

28.

Which begs the question: What is the Lungmotor? "The LUNG-MOTOR," explained the 1920 pamphlet, "is a simple and an easily understood device—always available—It is worked by hand—It can always give air, the kind you use everyday . . ."

29.

But what is it *really*? It is a pair of air pumps connected to a tube that is snaked down the victim's throat. It is a siphon of sorts, sucking the unwanted water up and out. "One of the great features of the LUNGMOTOR is the ease of operation," the pamphlet explained. "Anyone can operate the device . . . All the operator does is set the pin to the approximate size of the victim, cleanse mouth, pull out tongue, apply mask, and operate the device. Simple, isn't it? Nothing to watch but the patient."

30.

Simple, isn't it? Mengele thought as he conjoined the twins. *Nothing to watch but the patient.*

31.

Simple, isn't it? Schafer thought as he drowned the dogs. *Nothing to watch but the patient.*

32.

Simple, isn't it? Carrier thought as he drowned the priests. *Nothing to watch but the patient.*

33.

It is a misconception that when water enters the lungs of a drowning victim the lungs themselves drown. In fact, when the lungs are removed from a drowning victim and placed in water, the lungs remain buoyant. They float. What can this be but witchcraft?

34.

Water, sometimes, is a source of relief. If you are thirsty, for instance, or uncomfortably warm. It was a relief, also, for the boy at the summer camp whose body refused to bend. Brain damage kept him rigid, so I propped him against my chest in the lake—held him as close as I'd ever held anyone—and we rocked there, allowing the water to turn us weightless.

35.

The water burned from Shelley's body in the pyre. Bones cracked in the heat, brains boiled, and as Shelley's boatman burned, Lord Byron retreated once more to the sea. Took his walrus frame and just swam and to hell with the cramps. While Byron floundered, Trelawny claimed to have kept the vigil himself, later providing the primary account of the remains of Shelley's remains. "The only portions that were not consumed were some fragments of bones, the jaw, and the skull," Trelawny wrote, "but what surprised us all, was that the heart remained entire."

36.

I wonder: At the conclusion of his experiments, what were Josef Mengele's findings on the human heart?

37.

Have I told you of the time my wife, dog, and I ran into a stranger on the riverbank? How we had a nice chat as we stood there alongside the shore? How our conversation had consisted mostly of small talk, though when I casually asked if there were any updates

on the drowned boy, he casually said that no, they had yet to retrieve his nephew.

38.

The Lungmotor pamphlet comes to the following conclusion:
"Depending upon someone else to provide protection without
your personal assistance will not result in action. Everyone's
responsibility is the responsibility of no one. You realize, therefore, that the responsibility rests with each individual, and when
a death that could have been prevented occurs in your locality,
every individual is morally guilty . . ."

39.

Which raises the question: When Noah set sail, were the giraffes
the last creatures to drown? Did he notice their bleating black
tongues as they begged for mercy amid the tides?

40.

We have been told the Flood was spurred by man's wickedness,
but what crime, precisely, did the giraffes commit? And why, once
Noah had sailed out of sight, could a merciful God not have performed a rescue, earned himself a medal or two?

41.

God performed no rescue in the Gulf of Spezia, either. As Shelley
sank, the atheist poet expected nothing more. Within days, the
God-fearing faithful employed Shelley's death as a repudiation of
his sinful beliefs. England's *The Courier* wrote: "Shelley, the writer
of some infidel poetry, has been drowned, *now* he knows whether
there is God or no."

42.

When the flame failed to consume Shelley's heart, waterlogged and broken as it was, Trelawny reached his hand into the pyre and retrieved it. Mengele would have been proud—a heart removed with no anesthetic.

43.

Though Emmett Till's body was ruined, his heart remained intact. The doctors pieced him back together the best they could. As people peered inside the casket at that broken boy whose face was no longer his face, they felt everything. Someone with a camera snapped a photo, allowing us to see our own faces refracted back. That was the point. No anesthetic for any of us.

44.

If a river travels west at X miles per hour, and a body in that river travels at the same speed, what then were Emmett Till's last words?

45.

None of the aforementioned information will assist you if you are drowning.

Buckethead

Once a boy drowned at a summer camp. This was June of 1968.
It was early evening, a dinner of fried chicken and green beans
already breaking down inside the boys' bellies, and as their
counselors shouted numbers to the sky ("98 ... 99 ... 100!"), the
campers hid, determined not to be found in the all-camp game of
hide-and-seek.

More determined than most, ten-year-old Bobby Watson
slipped away from his bunkmates and wandered toward the floating docks on the shores of Blackman Lake. He blocked the sun
with his hand, allowing his eyes to refocus on the best hiding
spot of all. There, glistening at the edge of a dock, was a Kenmore
refrigerator. It was powder blue, round-topped, complete with
silver handle. Bobby—smitten perhaps by the peculiarity of a
refrigerator in such a strange locale—headed toward it.

Bobby knew as well as everyone else that the waterfront was off-limits to campers except during open swim. The head life-guard—a broad-shouldered, sunburned man—had made this abundantly clear on the first night of camp ("You do, you die"). But it was a game of hide-and-seek, after all, and Bobby, a boy who wanted simply to hide, convinced himself to duck beneath the peeling fence. He jogged toward the fridge, peeking behind him to make sure he hadn't been spotted. He hadn't. No sign of him except for footprints in the sand.

He reached for the shiny handle, pulled, listened for the sound of the door yawning open:

Click.

And then, after entering inside, the sound of the door closing:

Click.

The inner shelves had been removed, though it was still a tight squeeze for a boy Bobby's size. Nevertheless, he found that if he tucked himself into the fetal position, it almost felt like a womb. Somewhere in the world beyond the confines of that fridge, the dock wobbled beneath the new weight. Bobby smiled to himself. The boy who wanted simply to hide was quite certain they'd never find him.

Half an hour later, as the game wound down, Bobby's predic-tion proved true.

Baaaahhhhh-beeeeeee, the counselors' voices droned, followed by the sharper *Bob-be!*

Amidst the shouting, a maintenance man spotted the fridge on the dock and, in an uncharacteristic act, decided not to put off till tomorrow what could easily be done today. Rope in hand, he wandered toward the water, ducking beneath the paint-peeling fence as his work boots clomped toward the dock. He tied one end of a rope around the fridge and the other to the dock post.

The fridge was meant to serve as an anchor to ensure the docks didn't float away, and after the maintenance man double-checked his knots ("This'll hold"), he leaned his stocky frame into the powder-blue box and knocked it into the water.

Nobody knows what Bobby thought as that fridge bobbed twice in the lake. We can imagine, of course. How the water wiggled through the seams like eels. And how it began filling that fridge within seconds, drenching Bobby's shoes, Bobby's socks, Bobby's shorts. Meanwhile, on the other side of that refrigerator door, the maintenance man wiped his hands on his sleeves and headed toward the barn. There was a lawnmower in need of tuning.

Back on land, the counselors continued their search.

Baaaahhhhh-beeeeeee! they cried. *Come out, come out, wherever you are!*

A chorus of prepubescent campers soon joined them.

Hey, Bobby! Game over! Ollie ollie oxen free!

Inside the fridge, the water continued to rise. Past Bobby's orange-and-gray-striped T-shirt, past his slender neck, and finally, as the wide-eyed boy ballooned his cheeks for the last time, past his mouth and nose as well. His hands reached for a handle that was not there, his fingers clawing against the smooth surface. Then, as his cheeks deflated, he just stopped clawing. Just stopped everything. The refrigerator had become a coffin, and in the coming days, as a platoon of sheriff's deputies commandeered fishing boats and skimmed the water, nobody thought to tug on the rope pulled tight to the post of the dock. Nobody thought. Instead, those deputies took solace in the sound of their outboard motors, while Bobby—once a boy—became an anchor.

That night, as the campers slept or tried to, the counselors snuck from their cabins, slipped beneath the paint-peeling fence, and joined the head lifeguard at the waterfront. They were all so terribly young—most of them not yet twenty—and death, for them, was still an abstraction. As they tugged their damp swimsuits over their hips the goose bumps served as proof that they were alive.

"All right, let's link up," the head lifeguard called, so the counselors did—locking elbows to form a chain of boys whose high-kneed march plunged their toes deep into the sand. Their toes revealed no bodies that night, but thirty feet away and ten feet below, Bobby Watson's body responded to their ripples.

The days passed like seasons—the seasons like lifetimes—but first, the world stubbornly continued. That week's batch of campers returned home, while the next batch arrived soon after, dragging their trunks along the cabins' plywood floors. In the time between, the maintenance man mowed a lawn, patched a roof, installed a new refrigerator in the mess. When the new campers arrived, the counselors knew better than to talk about Bobby. Though the boys kept inquiring what all those sheriff's deputies were doing bobbing about in the water, the counselors remained mum, except for the one who lightened the mood by making some joke about bank-robbing bass.

The head lifeguard, too, spent the following week staring out at the boats from his place at the edge of the dock. The summer was blazing then, and every half an hour or so he'd reach for a white bucket, fill it with lake water, and send the water sizzling across the scalding docks. He repeated this action—a kind of keening—though one afternoon, as he walked to the boathouse to retrieve the goose poop broom, he returned to the dock to find his bucket missing.

This is the part of the story that gets gruesome, the part that, forty years later, when I am a counselor there myself, we are encouraged not to tell.

How, according to lore, that bucket didn't just disappear, but was taken—by Bobby—whose body had broken free from the fridge, though it was hardly his body any longer. His bones were intact, and most of his skin, though the fish had fed on his face.

A week after his disappearance, young Bobby—trapped in some transitory state (not quite dead, certainly not living)—was said to have broken his seaweed-speckled hand across the waterline and retrieved the bucket, slipping it over his fish-eaten face to spare others the view.

All of this, we told our campers by flashlight, *might have been different had Bobby just followed the rules. But he didn't. He just didn't. And that was the end of him.*

Before serving as a camp counselor, I was a camper, and for a week each summer I'd unfurl my sleeping bag on a hard mattress in the Apache cabin, unpack my sunscreen and calamine lotion, and begin using words like "kindling" and "rucksack" and "bug juice." Each week, our counselor told us the tale of Buckethead, reminding us of the importance of never wandering into the waterfront unattended ("You do, you die").

Years later, when I became counselor of that cabin, I began leading my own tribe of rucksack-carrying, bug-juice-drinking, kindling-finding boys. And I repeated the Buckethead legend as it had been told to me; adding a few flourishes, of course, including the pencil-scrawled initials "B. W." on one of the bunks to prove that Bobby Watson, too, had been an Apache. A necessary detail, I thought, to connect us with our fabricated past.

I probably took it too far—provided too many details on what it might feel like for water to rise in a confined space. Yet I told myself that my vivid recounting was meant merely to reinforce the cautionary tale; that if I told it well enough—true enough—I might scare these kids back to the safety of the shoreline.

During my second summer as a camper, I, too, was scared for my own good. I'd been scared the previous summer as well, and as I slipped my duffel beneath the familiar bunk once more, my hand grazed a white bucket tilted sideways like a bowling pin. I reached for it, though I stopped when I heard a cane slap the plywood floor behind me.

My eyes followed the cane up to the blind boy carrying it. He said hello ("Hi!), his name was Dennis ("I'm Dennis!"), and wondered whether he'd found his way into the Apache cabin.

It was the first time any of us had ever seen a blind boy, and my bunkmates and I wanted to know how he kept from tripping over all those roots in the path leading up to the cabin.

"Hell, I trip over shit all the time," announced Randall, the kid on the bunk above me. This, I later reasoned, might have been Randall's only glimpse of empathy, though our counselor misread it, told the kid to watch his damn mouth ("Or else").

That night, after a campfire spent fending off mosquitoes, the Apache tribe marched back through the woods to our cabin. Our counselor promised us a scary story if we could get in our sleeping bags without playing too much grab-ass ("Randall, Paul, I'm talking to you!").

We wanted the story so we did as we were told, peeling off sweat-soaked socks and shirts and curling—like Bobby—into spaces that were nearly too small for us. With the lights off, he told us about Buckethead, about Bobby Watson, about the refrigerator that clicked shut and did not open.

Since I knew the story, I mostly just watched the expressions on the other boys' faces. Across from me, Dennis's eyes emitted terror, but not nearly as much as Randall's.

"What a crock of shit," Randall grumbled, wadding up his pillow, though the tremor in his throat was unmistakable.

The week dragged on—days spent shooting bows and threading lanyards and trying to steer our canoes to the safety of the shoreline. We learned songs and then forgot them, built fires and put them out. We dedicated hours to sand volleyball, took turns at tetherball, measured the arc of our piss streams by the cattails.

Dennis couldn't take part in everything, but most of us did what we could to make him feel a part of our tribe. We took turns sitting next to him at dinner, trying hard to anticipate his needs, our eyes focused on the eyes that couldn't focus on us.

A few days in, Randall said something to Dennis—don't ask me what, it was all so long ago. Nevertheless, I remember feeling that his comment had seemed unnecessarily cruel, spiteful even, and though we were just innocent boys back then—still scared by the minnows that nipped our toes—we knew we had to retaliate.

Later that day, while Dennis slapped his cane along the blacktop, four of us sprawled ourselves on the lodge porch plotting against Randall. We knew Buckethead was his weakness, so we figured we'd scare him. We wanted him to feel cruelty, too.

As we tried to figure out how, I offhandedly mentioned the bucket beneath my bunk.

"What kind of bucket?" asked Paul.

"The right kind," I whispered.

That night, after campfire, we marched through the woods to the shower house as we'd done every night that week. We were an awkward bunch—some of us less suited for the wilderness than others ("Something bit my butt!")—and our three-minute trek always seemed to stretch on much longer. Somebody (usually me) was always dropping his shower caddy in the leaves, or getting his towel stuck in the craggy arms of the branches. That night, I broke a spider web with my face and felt terrible for what I'd done to that poor creature.

Who knows where our counselor was, probably attending to a scraped knee or a poison ivy outbreak. Years later, when I was the counselor, I could confirm that these injuries were endless, that it was impossible for nine-year-old boys not to sprain ankles or stumble into wasp nests. Whatever our counselor's alibi, it meant we were momentarily alone in that shower house, our mud-caked shoes tromping against the moldy tiles while we bit back guilty grins. The overhead lights gave us shadows, while a screened window invited in the summer heat. It was not hard to imagine decades of summers of boys just like us being baptized beneath those showerheads. Or if not there, then in the lake, or the mud, or half-drowned in the smoke around those campfires. I have seen black-and-white photographs from those ancient times, pictures of boys in war paint who—with the exception of Bobby (if there ever was a Bobby)—were lucky enough to grow to become old men.

Yet we thought little of history or our place in it as we kicked our clothes into a pile and positioned ourselves beneath those showerheads. We thought little of the story we would become.

Our thoughts remained on Randall as he snapped a towel or two our way ("Take that, suckers!"). We did. We took it. He would get his soon enough.

A light flickered, a bug zapped, and I began reciting my line.

"Guys," I said rather unconvincingly. "I think I saw Buckethead out the window."

Refusing to look himself, Randall pretended to study the soap in his washcloth.

"Did you?" asked Dennis, reaching for my arm.

"Aw, he didn't see jack shit," Randall said.

"Then look," someone pressed. "Why don't you look?"

Newly emboldened, Randall marched bare-assed toward the screen and peeked out.

"See? Nothing out there but . . ."

We killed the lights as Paul pounded his plastic head against the shower house screen. His moans were louder than ours, more desperate, how I imagined a sheep might sound in the final thrusts of labor. I couldn't see Paul's face behind the bucket, but I thought of Bobby's, what his might've looked like had his tragedy been true.

Randall screamed—it was all we wanted from him—so we flicked on the lights and told Paul to remove his bucket.

But what we saw with the lights on was far worse than what Randall had seen with them off:

Dennis—our friend, our charge—curled naked on the mossy tiles.

We'd underestimated the effect of confusion on a blind boy.

"Hey, Dennis, it was no one," I said, hovering over him. "We were trying to teach a lesson." The others gathered around him, touching his shoulder and his forehead to let him know they were there.

Dennis kept shaking, and as we repeatedly asked if he was all right—if he'd pull through—he just kept shaking, not quite a yes or a no.

Who can remember what happened on the walk back to the cabin that night? Randall shut his foul mouth for a change—I remember that much—and a pair of us may have threaded our arms through Dennis's as we led him back through the woods.

That night, for the first time, we went to bed without talking.

"Finally tuckered you out," our counselor said upon his return. "About time."

While the others slept, I became newly afraid of the dark. I'd never needed a nightlight before, though I needed one then—the sliver of moon refracting off the lake seemed suddenly insufficient. Still, I took comfort where I could, reminding myself that the bucket was back beneath my bunk, that for the moment it wasn't hiding anyone's flesh-eaten face.

The box fan on the windowsill out-hummed the crickets, but I still knew they were out there, chirping as Buckethead's sea-weeded shoes dragged along the overgrown trails. My imagination conjured him so clearly—a boy more scared than scary grasping in the dark, hoping for something to touch or to touch him.

Across from me, Dennis lay in his bunk, his hands folded across his chest. I couldn't tell if he was awake or not, if he was afraid or not, so I balanced on my elbow to have a look.

"Hey, you still up?" I whispered. He didn't answer.

But his eyes, like mine, were wide.

The Changing

You are twenty-one and preparing to change your first diaper.

This is not how you imagined it might go.

You are a counselor at a summer camp in a midwestern state, and the boy in need of changing is not your son. Years later, when you have a son yourself, you will better understand the intricacies of the process—how half the trick to diaper changing is keeping the kid from squirming.

But on this day, there will be no squirming. This boy could not squirm if he tried.

During the flag lowering, a fellow counselor whispers, *The boy in the Med Shed requires assistance.*

You nod. You believe you can handle it.

Already this summer, you have surprised yourself by handling all sorts of things—driving a tractor, a pontoon, a pickup truck. You have kept campers safe as they scaled towers, roasted weenies, and cannonballed into the lake.

What's so hard, you wonder, *about changing a diaper?*

Once the flag is folded and properly stowed you make your way toward the Med Shed. You enter, open the door to the room on the left, and stare at the fifteen-year-old boy lying limp in his bunk. Only he is not limp. He is the opposite of limp. Rigid. Solid. Statuesque. A narrow rail that twists. His eyes flitter toward you, and you wonder if he wonders if you know why you are here.

You know why, of course, and since you don't want to embarrass him, you don't try to act like this is nothing, like this is something you have done a million times before. You haven't (this much is obvious to you both), and you want to spare the boy the indignity of your act.

To your left are the diapers, and you feel your hand reaching toward them. Now one is in your hand.

Good, you think, *halfway there.*

But as soon as you pull your hand toward the boy you realize the logistics are lost on you. Your body stiffens, imitating his own. Surely there is some protocol for this sort of thing, but no one has ever filled you in on the details. There was no mention of this anywhere in your counselor's training manual, and when you think back to the Red Cross–sponsored babysitting class of your youth, all you remember is that the practice dolls felt as inflexible as this boy.

You can feel his eyes on you now—doubting you, testing you— so you turn your back to him and scan the diaper bag for directions. There are none. Or at least none you understand. Changing a diaper, it appears, is as simple as folding an origami swan with both hands behind your back.

(Which is bad news for people like you who can barely fold the flag.)

From your place inside the Med Shed you hear the voices of children whose bodies were not born rigid. As if to prove it, they burst past the window, a stampede of limber legs kicking up dust. You can hardly blame them for their ignorance. And yet . . .

Would it kill them, you wonder, to consider the boy who cannot stampede?

This is not cruelty, you know, just kids being kids. And yet . . .

Might it seem cruel, you wonder, to the boy on the bunk?

You consider scolding them—*Keep it down! Knock it off with all that racket!*—but ultimately you don't. You don't even close the window.

Maybe, you think, he likes racket.

You will stay with that boy throughout the evening and much of the following day. He and you, you and him, you are inseparable.

Why you? Because the better counselor got sick and you are the next best thing.

But also because you're falling in love with your boss—who happens also to be that sick counselor's sister—which is why you volunteered in the first place.

You want desperately to portray yourself as an empathetic care-giver—a suitable spouse—and this boy gives you that chance.

Fast-forward a few years, and you and that sick counselor's sister will wed just a hundred yards from that Med Shed, your guests circling the fire pit where you once sang ten thousand campfire songs. Tucked tight in your tux, you'll stare out at them and see the ghost faces of campers whose names you now forget. And as you take your vows alongside the lake ("in sickness and in health"), not once will that boy cross your mind.

After showers but before lights out, a smaller stampede of half-busted boys makes its way toward the Med Shed. When they enter—complaining of bites and bruises and poison ivy—the creak of the door makes sleep impossible for that boy who sweats stone-faced in his sheets.

One after another, the campers come in search of cures for their momentary ailments.

I was running through the oak grove, one boy tells the nurse, *when I was attacked by a swarm of mosquitoes . . .*

I was running, he repeats, which hardly sounds like an ailment to the boy in the bunk who never has.

The nurse keeps an endless supply of calamine lotion, Gold Bond, and Popsicles, and somehow these are the only cures those boys ever seem to require.

Freshly healed (and with purple Popsicles dangling from their lips) the campers begin their long walks back to their cabins.

Out your room's window, you and the boy can just make out their small shadows pushing against the dark. Eventually, you hear what appears to be dillydallying ("Dude! Check out this bug!"), so you shout for the boys to double-time it back to their bunks.

"I'll time you," you call out the window. "1 . . . 2 . . . 3 . . ."

The fuse is lit, the campers run, their tennis shoes skimming the earth.

You turn from the window to watch the boy staring hard at the wooden bunk above him, his twig legs crisscrossed at the ankles.

"Hey, want me to close this?" you ask, nodding to the window.

His face is immutable: dark eyes, aquiline nose, slightly sunken cheeks.

"Maybe we'll close it this time," you say, and when you see no reaction—not even the flittering of eyes—you reach your hands toward the pane and press down.

The following day—your last day together—proves to be a scorcher. It's so hot, in fact, that not even all the shade from all the oak trees in the grove can adequately protect you. Water is the only relief the camp has to offer, and so all activities are cancelled. All campers are to report directly to the lake with their sunscreen.

All the campers but one.

From your place inside the Med Shed, you and the boy hear a bleating "Marco!" followed by "Polo!" You and the boy hear the aftermath of the cannonballs as those campers fold their knees to their chests.

You offer an apologetic smile, as if to say, *Hey, I get it. I'm an empathetic guy.*

But you both know you don't get it.

Don't get what it's like to be held captive by your body, to be forced to hold a pose indefinitely.

During rest hour—when the rest of the campers return to their sweltering cabins to write letters home ("The food is great! The lake is great! We love it!")—you and the boy decide to go for a dip.

It's just a lake, you think, *what could possibly go wrong?*

You follow one step behind as the boy hums his power chair down the path that leads to the water. He stops his chair just short of the sand, which is when you enter the scene.

You lift his small frame from his chair and carry him toward the water, cupping one hand beneath his knobby knees and the other beneath his back. Each bead of sweat clings to him, obscuring his face and collecting in his cheeks.

In that moment, all you want in the world is to give that boy what he wants. Somebody has told you he likes the water, and since you are in a position to give him that, you do.

From his place at the shaded picnic table, the lifeguard spots you headed his way.

He asks if he can help and you say sure, then you split the boy's weight between you.

As the three of you enter the lake, you convince yourself that a boy like him must like buoyancy. That a boy in his condition must like the way the water turns everything weightless. Removes friction, eases grating, allows a body to rock in the waves.

Years later, you will all but forget those waves, that water, the whir of the air conditioner in the Med Shed. What you will remember most is the changing. How you struggled to work the angles as you pulled that diaper down. How his knees had proven too sharp, and how each time you spread his legs they snapped back like a bear trap newly sprung.

Back in those days, you were just some boy and he was just some boy, but when you finally do grow up and have a son yourself, every diaper change will seem easy in comparison.

At last you learn the protocol—not from any counselor's manual, or any babysitting class—but from the sick counselor's sister, your wife of three years, who turns your son's legs to Play-Doh in her hands. For a thousand diapers you'll observe the way she squeezes his ankles together with a single hand and wipes, singing a campfire song while she does it.

You will repeat this because it is the simplest way you know to show love—unmistakable, irrefutable, your pact.

Death by Refrigerator

When inventor Oliver Evans first conceived of his "refrigeration machine" in 1805, he never dreamed it could be a killer. He, much like Jacob Perkins and John Gorrie (both of whom would soon improve upon the design), dreamed simply of extending the preservation properties of food. None of them imagined their invention had deadly potential, providing a perfect-sized trap for a curious child who dared step inside.

I first learned of refrigerator deaths while serving as a camp counselor in a small country town in Indiana. The victim was a boy named Bobby Watson, who in the summer of 1968—while lost in the throes of a game of hide-and-seek—wedged himself into an abandoned fridge left to rust on the edge of the dock. A maintenance man wandered past moments later, tied the fridge to the dock, and heaved it into the water, wholly unaware of the child hiding within.

The fridge, we informed our campers during weekly retellings, *was meant to serve as an anchor for the docks, though for Bobby it served as a coffin instead.*

I dedicated several summers to this place and can verify the story. That is, I can verify that it *is* a story, one employed by counselors as a cautionary tale to scare campers into steering clear of the waterfront after dark. Yet no matter how well we told it (and most of us told it quite well), the campers always seemed far less afraid of drowning than the other half of the horror: being trapped inside that fridge.

If a boy named Bobby Watson did actually die inside a refrigerator in 1968, he was hardly the first. From the 1930s through the 1960s, America's refrigerator deaths occurred with surprising regularity. Although there's no verifiable truth to Bobby Watson's tale—no newspaper reports or camp records confirm his existence—the story was likely inspired by the multitude of other deaths that occurred in similar fashion.

By the 1950s the death-by-refrigerator epidemic became a public health concern—albeit a strange one—and in response to the crisis, in August of 1956 Congress passed the Refrigerator Safety Act. The legislation required that refrigerators be designed to open from the inside, and made it illegal for shippers to transport any unit that failed to meet this standard. The act—while an important first step—did not immediately solve the problem. There were still far too many unsafe refrigerators in operation, and the government could do little to force citizens to replace their perfectly functional fridges. In the years to come—as compressors and fans overheated—thousands of refrigerators were disposed of, though not always responsibly.

"At least 163 [refrigerator] deaths were reported nationwide between 1956 and 1964," reports writer Cecil Adams, adding that the number climbed even higher in the mid-1960s before eventually leveling off and falling as the newer, safer models replaced the old. Nevertheless, the tragedies continued, prompting the press (and camp counselors) to maintain focus on the problem by immortalizing this peculiar fraternity of children whose curiosity ultimately cost them their lives.

Children like three-year-old Larry Murphy and his four-year-old cousin Paul, who in June of 1954 were discovered by a junkman as he prepared to break up an abandoned refrigerator in New London, Connecticut.

They say Bobby's mouth was full of fishes.

Or children like four-year-old Cynthia Ann Hartman and older brothers Joseph (five) and Martin (six), all of whom managed to squeeze themselves inside an empty fridge in Chicago in August of '64.

No one knows how long Bobby lasted until the air ran out.

Three years later, in July of '67, Roger L. Brown—who, according to the newspaper, had previously "been warned by his parents about playing in or around the abandoned refrigerator behind their house"—failed to heed that warning. He was found suffocated inside a fridge in Sarasota, Florida.

Fully aware of the threat refrigerators posed, in July of 1976 the Herrig & Herrig Insurance Company placed an ad in a Dubuque newspaper in which they—much like we camp counselors—employed fear as a deterrent for death. "It doesn't take long for these tightly insulated refrigeration units to snuff out a life," the ad began. "A child becomes unconscious in ten minutes and dies within twenty-five minutes." In its haunting conclusion, the ad also notes, "And don't assume that magnetic doors are childproof. Many children will just curl up and go to sleep once inside."

The image of children peacefully curled up inside refrigerators seemed in stark contrast to the death Bobby Watson endured. His experience—fictional as it was—was nothing short of a fingernail-clawing horror story, an account that likely shared many details with the real-life tales. However, more shocking than either the vividness of the insurance ad or the Watson story was the realization that these tragedies could have been easily prevented had the public followed proper disposal protocol. To ensure the mistake was never repeated (again), the media issued a call for action, with one newspaper deeming refrigerators "child traps," while another described them as a "menace."

Forget Evans's, Perkins's, and Gorrie's great strides in the advancement of food preservation; for the moment, refrigerators were little more than chambers of death for the innocent.

A coffin-sized home for Bobby Watson.

In 1985, UCLA epidemiologist Dr. Jeff Kraus released a study, "Effectiveness of Measures to Prevent Unintentional Deaths of Infants and Children from Suffocation and Strangulation," that provided an in-depth look at the 471 lethal cases reported in California between 1960 and 1981. When Kraus broke the number down further, it revealed that plastic garment bags were the primary suffocative child killer (responsible for 109 deaths), while refrigerators came in second with 84. As a result of both federal and state legislative efforts, Kraus reported a sharp decline in suffocation and strangulation deaths, though many were left to wonder how such a seemingly innocuous kitchen appliance—one used several times a day—had become such a safety hazard.

Some might argue that our discomfort with refrigerator deaths centered not on the deaths themselves, but on the complexity of our new relationship with the machine. In the early twentieth century, refrigerators quickly became America's most necessary appliance—our protector of sustenance—though they soon revealed their ability to take life away as well. It must have felt like a betrayal of sorts; after all our years of feeding from it, it appeared to be feeding on us.

Though, of course, we can't overlook the terror the grief-stricken parents felt upon imagining their child's death, a trauma that was better preserved in their heads than the food inside their fridges. Parents couldn't help but wonder what it might be like for their child to struggle from the inside, pounding hard at a door that simply would not give. The problem with the old refrigerators, Cecil Adams explained, was that their design "prevented air from getting in and the kids' screams from getting out."

What could possibly be more terrifying than that?

People fear any number of things, only some of which make logical sense. Nevertheless, we have a name for all of them. If you fear bellybuttons, then you suffer from omphalophobia. If you fear kitchen appliances (including the fridge), then you are an oikophobic. We have even given a name to those who fear nothing but the possibility of procuring a fear: they are phobophobics.

According to psychologist Nandor Fodor, claustrophobia—a fear from which Bobby Watson apparently did not suffer until his fatal moments—is defined as the "widespread morbid dread of confined spaces, small rooms, caves, tunnels, elevators, or pressing crowds." Dr. Robert Campbell later revised the definition to include additional claustrophobia-inducing locales ("theaters, classrooms, boats, or narrow streets").

Neither definition makes mention of refrigerators.

If you were to ask a sufferer of claustrophobia to name additional omissions, he might mention cellars, airplanes, cars, churches, roller coasters, or the daily fear of wearing a necktie.

Imagine being buried alive in a hole. It's like that.

While the majority of mid-twentieth-century psychologists could easily diagnose the phobia, they struggled to gauge the degree to which a patient suffered. As a result, in 1979 psychologists developed the claustrophobia scale, a twenty-question assessment that deduced the acuteness of one's fear. Participants were asked to rate their anxiety or avoidance on a number of uncomfortable scenarios, including "entering a windowless lavatory and locking the door," "riding a small elevator by yourself," and "being outdoors in a fog when you can only see a few yards in front of you."

Once more, refrigerators were left off the scale.

When tracing claustrophobia's roots, Nandor Fodor looked first to one's true beginning: birth. In his 1949 book, *The Search for the Beloved: A Clinical Investigation of the Trauma of Birth and Pre-Natal Conditioning,* Fodor provides an in-depth description of the brief yet horrifying moment all newborns share; the moment in which the child must take his or her first breath independent of the mother. "If this interval is too prolonged, the baby will turn blue and suffocate," Fodor explains. "If the baby lives to breathe, it has tasted death by suffocation."

While few claim to remember this post-birth near-death experience, Fodor argues that the psychological stress of the moment is forever encoded in the subconscious, that "evidence of it can be found in morbid suffocation fears." For Fodor, our fear of confined spaces (and the possibility of suffocating within them) is simply an unavoidable side effect of being born, one that points toward an inarguable truth: before we can breathe, we can't.

While an estimated 5–7 percent of the world suffers from claustrophobia, far fewer suffer from its little-known counterpart, claustrophilia—which Dr. Robert Campbell defines as the "pathological desire to be confined and enclosed within a small space." Confirming Fodor's work, Campbell adds that claustrophilia is often "interpreted psychoanalytically as an escape from the world and a tendency to return to the womb."

He could only hold his breath for so long.

If claustrophobia serves as a psychological reminder that our mothers' wombs are one-way swinging doors, sufferers of claustrophilia might well argue the opposite. While claustrophobia can be acquired at birth or developed later in life, claustrophilia seems to be a biological imperative of birth. It's as if, in the early stages of development, Fodor's theory of birth trauma as a gateway to claustrophobia remains momentarily repressed, at least for newborns, who remain the world's most exuberant practitioners of the claustrophilic life. An industry of baby care books seems to confirm this, including Dr. Harvey Karp's parental favorite, *The Happiest Baby on the Block,* which also argues that babies much prefer the tight wrap of a swaddle to the freedom of unrestrained sleep.

Karp's theory proved particularly true for my then-four-month-old son, whom we tucked tight in a swaddle and inserted into an MRI machine on the University of Wisconsin–Madison campus. He wasn't ill, but had simply been selected for a psychological study. Since a trusted friend promised to administer the test, my wife and I signed off on the experiment.

Despite our efforts, we couldn't swaddle him tight enough to alleviate his fear, nor could I blame him for having it. After all, if my own helpless body had been folded and inserted into a cylindrical tube, I, too, would have cried. But eventually the swaddle did its work, his mother and I keeping careful watch as his wails subsided and he returned to a womblike state. We witnessed no trauma, just contentment, though as he slept, I began feeling claustrophobic on his behalf. I took a seat in a nearby rocking chair and watched as the red glowing numbers kept track of his heartbeat like a basketball score in flux. I rocked to that heartbeat, the quick back and forth of the chair a small comfort as I prayed for him to stay asleep.

Bobby was awake for all of it, conscious and clawing as the water wiggled through the seams like eels.

As I rocked there, I couldn't help but wonder about the long-lasting ramifications of this trial, if we might forever scar him if he woke while trapped inside the tube.

He did wake eventually, breathless as he struggled to break free from the straitjacket in which we'd enclosed him. Our psychologist friend immediately shut the experiment down, pressing the red button that eased the magnets back into place, killing the buzzing and whirring that had engulfed us all moments prior. The damage was done, though we hoped nothing was permanent. Not as it had been for the fictional Bobby Watson—or far worse—for the real-life Larry and his cousin Paul, for Cynthia and her brothers Joseph and Martin, all of whom drowned above water.

We left the lab and did not return there.

We don't swaddle him anymore; he doesn't let us.

If we were to be subjected to a bombing attack, what
type bombs would probably be used against us?

"Questionnaire Used at Meeting of Residents Residing in
Zone 2, District 1, Section #2, Ft. Wayne" (1942)

III.
DROPPED

Fabricating Fear

We searched for a lake monster on the shores of Lake Superior. This was in July of 2012. My wife, Meredith, son Henry, and I had headed north from Eau Claire, Wisconsin, in the hope that the vacation town of Duluth, Minnesota, might momentarily insulate us from the horrors of the world.

It didn't.

Didn't drown out the drone missiles dropped in Pakistan or silence the Syrian uprising.

In the days prior to our trip, I'd found I could hardly turn on the television without learning of the latest in a long line of disasters—flash floods in Russia, drought in West Africa, a car bombing in Kandahar. Not to mention an earthquake in New Zealand and Ireland's torrential rains. For days on end, cable news had little trouble confirming that every last vestige of the planet was crumbling or washing away, bombed or broken or both.

Except, of course, Duluth.

By the time we arrived at Minnesota Point beach, we were disheartened to find that we'd already lost most of the daylight. Still, I kept my six-month-old son confined to the safety of the shore by using what little light remained to search for monsters.

"Keep your eyes peeled for an arched neck," I said as we sat in the sea grass, "or a couple of dark humps in the water."

Henry knew little of lake monsters, though his cryptid-loving father knew plenty.

I filled him in the best I could, but Henry's interest had little to do with the lake or the creatures that may or may not inhabit it. Instead, he focused on the sand, deemed it edible, and proceeded to sprinkle it into his mouth.

Sighing, I put our monster hunt on hold to deal with more pressing matters.

"We'll try again tomorrow," I said, scraping the sand from his tongue.

Surely the monsters would wait for us.

Was it Dr. Spock who said parents should scare the living daylights out of their kids in order to expose them to fear? Perhaps I misunderstood. Nevertheless, I manufactured our lake monster hunt for the same reason my family has instilled fear into offspring for generations—because much in the way a flu shot works, we believe a small dose of fear in a controlled environment is far safer than the alternative.

Though I fancy myself a fiction writer, my mother's fictions were always best, especially her creation of Mr. Green—a much-feared, nonexistent neighbor who terrified both my brother and me throughout our childhoods. We never so much as glimpsed the guy, knew startlingly little about him, yet the mysterious Mr. Green became the manifestation of everything that scared us. Our imaginations concocted a creature so vile, so cruel, that we never dared cross my mother for fear she'd make good on her bluff to introduce us to the man.

Except for the time my brother did cross her.

Who can remember his transgression? All I know is that the punishment could hardly have fit the crime. I watched helplessly from the windows of our Fort Wayne, Indiana, home as she buckled him into the backseat of the Ford Taurus and drove toward Mr. Green's supposed house.

My brother later recounted all of it. How our mother pulled into Mr. Green's alleged driveway, turned off the engine, and waited.

And how as he sweated bullets in the backseat, my brother prayed to the God of little boys that Mr. Green might take pity on a wretch like him.

I'll never be bad again, I'll never be bad again, I'll never be bad again . . .

Miraculously, God answered.

My straight-faced mother had put on quite a performance, but just as my brother's anxiety reached its apex, she shrugged and reversed the car out of the drive.

"Looks like he's not home," my mother said, shaking a finger at my brother in the rearview. "You got lucky this time, mister."

As my son and I sat in the sea grass on that Sunday night in Duluth, I realized just how much I needed him to believe in our lake monster. I needed it the same way my mother needed us to believe in Mr. Green. I felt that if I could expose Henry to a tiny dose of a lesser fear, then I could shoulder the heavier burdens myself. And not just your everyday, run-of-the-mill global upheaval, but the more pressing matters, the threats that hit closer to home. Such as the burden of knowing that any number of once seemingly innocuous household objects—from bookshelves to coffee tables—take on a far more menacing role when a child's in the room. And the burden of recognizing that even if I did manage to beat the needle-in-a-haystack odds at successfully childproofing our child's life, it was impossible to childproof his future. There were simply not enough latches or plug covers or antibacterial soaps. Not enough bubble wrap, or water wings, or luck.

Despite teeth brushing, and hand washing, and practicing stop, drop, and roll, I would never be able to predict when the drunk driver might barrel into our lives. Nor would I know which dog would bark and which would bite and which of the two had rabies. Would never know which square of sidewalk would bloody the knee, or who would break whose heart in the schoolyard. I am not alone in my worry. All any parent can predict is that none of our children will ever be immune to everything, and that at some point, our years of nonstop parental anxieties might come to fruition just as we'd feared.

And so, for that brief moment in Duluth, I dreamed up a fear for him that I could still control. I assured myself that fabrication would serve Henry well down the road. That a lake monster would shield him from drone attacks and flash floods and car bombings in Kandahar. But more importantly, it might also make him think twice before leaping into the bacteria-filled lake, or choking down any more sandcastles. I was just being a pragmatist. Just a pragmatic, monster-hunting father.

My mother likely confirmed the value of her own parental indiscretions with similar rationalizations. Sure, a bit of minor therapy might be in order as a result of our Mr. Green–induced traumas, but wasn't it a necessary means to the end? Was it not better for her to frontload our fears rather than expose us to a larger dose of a harsher reality? After all, thanks to my Mr. Green anxiety, for several years I was able to naively believe that the two Gulf wars were fought exclusively with nine irons and putters. Ultimately, I was no worse off for my mostly bubble-wrapped childhood. I lifted the lighter load, while Mom bore the weight of the world.

That night on the beach, we saw no evil, we heard no evil, there was none; though months later, there was plenty of it all over the world. Televisions piped horrors into households from Duluth on down. Thankfully, Henry was still too young to know the difference between Sandy Hook and Hurricane Sandy and the sand he devoured in Duluth.

There will be plenty of time for differentiating later, I thought.

For now, when the news reports on the latest tragedy, Meredith and I carry our twenty-eight-pound boy to his bed and return him once more to the safety of his room.

On one particularly depressing news day, we take to his Legos and construct our Lake Superior monster, complete with arched neck and dark humps.

Henry laughs at our creation, and we laugh, too.

"We've found him!" I say. "We've found that scary scalawag at last!"

But the very next moment he's destroying that monster faster than a flash flood.

As we watch him, our stomachs drop as our own worst fear pulls into sharp focus: no matter how hard we try—or how much we love him—the fear we fake for him today might well turn true tomorrow.

Fort Wayne Is Still Seventh on Hitler's List

For Michael Martone

In the 1940s, citizens would tell you that Fort Wayne, Indiana, was so wrapped in magnetic wire, superchargers, sonar systems, bombshells, pistons, amplidynes, and dynamotors that for a brief moment the people there became important enough to fear obliteration. Employees at General Electric, Rea Magnet Wire Company, and International Harvester clocked in seven days a week to support the war effort, churning out all the necessary parts.

Without Fort Wayne, perhaps there would be no B-24 bomber.

Without Fort Wayne, perhaps there would be no atomic bomb.

When Little Boy was dropped over Hiroshima, a small piece of Fort Wayne was lodged inside. On Taylor Street, Joslyn Steel Manufacturing shaped uranium into ingots, contributing to the killing of 160,000 people 6,700 miles away.

Days later, when Fat Man was dropped over Nagasaki, once more Fort Wayne was to blame. Twenty-one-year-old assistant flight engineer Corporal Robert J. Stock of 415 Downing Street—just five miles from where I grew up—peered down from his instrument panel at the mushroom cloud ballooning thirty thousand feet below.

His mission: measure destruction.

Which he did, admirably, making him better prepared than most to know the effects of the bomb had Hitler dropped his own upon the steeples of the churches of Fort Wayne.

A handout from a May 18, 1942, citywide meeting responded to Fort Wayne citizens' questions on how to respond if Hitler bombed the city.

Q. Aside from ordinary fires due to combustion or any other natural source, do you feel there is any danger from fire that we might expect?

A. Yes there is another danger we must face now that we are at war. That danger is from enemy airplanes dropping incendiary bombs.

Q. What is an incendiary bomb?

A. It is a small bomb weighing about two pounds.

They burned at 4,500 degrees Fahrenheit.

In a coffee shop on Broadway, old men still talk about the planes humming over their city.

"Probably twenty or thirty of them," a retired mailman shrugs, sipping his coffee. "We had to look up and try to figure out if they were our planes or theirs. We were always waiting for the day when we saw a swastika on the back wing."

That day never came.

With their heads tilted skyward, they spied only skywriters or C-47s droning high above.

The only strike they ever knew was lightning.

In October of 1941, in the months prior to Pearl Harbor, Charles Lindbergh spoke to a crowd of ten thousand at the Gospel Temple on Rudisill Boulevard. His noninterventionist group, the America First Committee, was opposed to the American invasion of Europe and Lindbergh looked forward to sharing his feelings with Fort Wayne. The city was proud to host him, with onlookers crowding the streets and sidewalks to catch a glimpse. But in the early afternoon of December 7, 1941, as Fort Wayne citizens stepped from their churches and received word of the attack on Pearl Harbor, Lindbergh and his isolationist policy were quickly forgotten. The American First Committee disbanded within days while the men of Fort Wayne rushed to recruiting stations. Six hundred and twelve men who were raised on streets like Wayne and Sherman and Clay would die in places they never knew existed.

My father gets his oil changed at a service station on Covington Road.

"Eighteen bucks for the full service," he says. "You can't beat it."

Once, many years back, I attended Lindley Elementary with the owner's son. His name was Ryan, and for a time, our desks sat in the same row. During free-reading period, Ryan and I often hunkered into beanbag chairs that swallowed us whole, taking turns holding *The Illustrated Guide to Fossils,* pointing out which fossils we would most like to find on our way home from school. We had never heard of Hitler, nor had we ever been told that Fort Wayne—our beloved home—was important enough to make it to the top of any list.

"I want to find a trilobite," Ryan once told me, so I said, "Okay. I want to find one, too."

Nearly twenty years later, Ryan died. Small-arms fire from insurgents in Balad, Iraq. He was a corporal. He was a paratrooper. He was no longer in the beanbag chair beside me.

Once, during an oil change, my father asked his father how many tours his son had served. Ryan's father didn't speak, just held up his grease-stained fingers.

In the coffee shop on Broadway, just a few blocks from General Electric, old men still talk about the German prisoners of war.

"Probably thousands," the retired mailman continues. "I was just a little boy then, but we used to sit on my grandmother's porch and wave to them as they jogged by for their daily exercise."

Reports show that by 1945, six hundred German prisoners of war had infiltrated our city.

Camp Scott was originally constructed for the 130th Railroad Battalion, but by 1944, it had transformed to a prison camp. Guard towers were erected, barbed wire rolled out.

The camp was situated just beyond McMillen Park, between Wayne Trace and the Pennsylvania Railroad. The Germans were captured from Rommel's Afrika Korps before flying into Fort Wayne.

The men at the coffee shop recall Sunday afternoons spent driving past the camp, the prisoners peeking out from the fences.

Once the prisoners arrived, some parents no longer allowed their children outside after dark. But some parents did. There are stories of German POWs playing soccer in the park, of children accepting the prisoners' nickels to buy them sodas from nearby drugstores. The prisoners had access to radios and received more generous beer and cigarette rations than American soldiers overseas. They enjoyed Ping-Pong. They found girlfriends. They stuck around.

You ask them, they'll tell you—Fort Wayne is a good place to live.

The night after 353 Japanese aircraft attacked Pearl Harbor, the General Electric factory on Broadway turned off its glowing sign for the first time since 1928. The GE symbol had become a stalwart of the Fort Wayne skyline, but the red-encircled letters remained dark until war's end. Nine hundred and twenty-five bulbs quieted their hum, and six months later, GE produced its last civilian motor before focusing entirely on war production. Security fences were constructed around the factory, and employees were given high-level identification badges. Armed guards were stationed in guardhouses. The war had reached our backyard.

Nearby, at the Wolf and Dessauer department store on Calhoun Street, the forty thousand lights depicting a glowing Santa and sleigh flickered into darkness as well.

The citizens of Fort Wayne knew one thing for certain:

They did not want Santa Claus in the German crosshairs as the bombs began falling from the sky.

Cloistered in the backroom of Fort Wayne's History Center sits a gray box filled with various manila folders, one of which reads simply "Bombs." Inside, a list of the threats that Fort Wayne most likely faced, as well as information related to how citizens were to respond if Hitler bombed the city.

One pamphlet reminds Fort Wayne citizens that should they find themselves in a blackout, they are to remain calm, obey all traffic signals, and assist the infirm, the frightened, and the lost.

And remember, the pamphlet chides, "a blackout or air raid warning is a warning and not a promise of one."

Q. What usually happens when an incendiary bomb strikes a home?

A. It will penetrate the roof of any ordinary constructed home. The force of the contact will ignite it and the chemicals within the bomb itself will start working. It will generate heat at about 4700 degrees Fahrenheit. At that heat almost anything will burn.

Q. A lot of questions have arisen on air raids. What would you suggest as a first step in protecting yourself from an air raid?

A. Every person should select in his home a place that would be suitable for occupancy during an air raid. It has been suggested that a basement room is preferable for this purpose.

The Q&A also recommends that a radio, table, chairs, books, and magazines be kept in the basement, as there is no telling how long the bombing might continue. Newspapers described basements filled with water and nonperishable food; men preparing to darken the city at a moment's notice; air wardens stationed at the top of the Lincoln Tower, scanning the skies. Posters plastered to telephone poles and trolley cars, reminding citizens "Loose lips sink ships."

If the blackouts were done properly, even the posters would disappear.

Most blackouts were announced in advance, but not always. One flyer reads:

BLACK OUT

SUNDAY NIGHT

MAY 24, 1942

FROM 10 PM TO 10:15 PM

PLEASE FOLLOW THIS ONE RULE:

TURN OFF ALL LIGHTS DURING THIS PERIOD!

Yet in late May, the flyers were replaced with a confidential memo, one in which Carter Bowser of Fort Wayne's Command Control Center informed the Fort Wayne Police Department of a surprise blackout scheduled for June 4, 1942, from 9:30 PM until 9:45 PM. Bowser hoped the unannounced blackout might better simulate the conditions of a true bombing, might strike fear into Fort Wayne's citizenry by keeping them on full alert.

On June 4, a siren rang and light bulb filaments throughout the city rattled and died away. The trolleys stopped in the streets, their lights dimmed, while cars killed their engines. When Colonel Robert Harsh of the Office of Civilian Defense came to inspect Fort Wayne's preparedness, he left quite impressed by the city's ability to turn itself invisible, returning the land to fallow fields, the city to grids on a map.

A month later, an instructional film entitled *Bombs over Fort Wayne* premiered at the Murat Temple Theatre on New Jersey

Street in Indianapolis. Though the sixteen-millimeter film is lost, the original script remains.

> NARRATOR: It's a warm spring night in the city where three rivers meet. Late theatre-goers and workers have long since departed for their homes. A lone policeman patrols his beat. Far off—an automobile horn shatters the stillness of the night.

Then—silence, the city settling in for a night of rest.

Moments later, the calm of the Fort Wayne night is disrupted by the German air strike.

> CONTROLLER: High explosive bombs at Calhoun and Pontiac! Casualties approximately ten. Fire in three buildings. Electric wire down.

> POLICE: Enemy aircraft crashed through high tension wires at Delaware and Alabama. Some persons still in plane, some thrown out. Approximately six persons injured.

Incendiary bombs explode at the corner of Berry and Union as messenger boys are sent sprinting through streets.

> "Several enemy escaped from the plane and seen going east!" actors cry. "Several unexploded bombs scatter in vicinity. Some smell of gas!"

Bomb squads and decontamination teams enter the scene. Officers in riot gear chase after the six downed Germans as they scatter past the Embassy Theatre, their swastikas reflecting on their aviation suits.

By movie's end, it's clear that Fort Wayne's quick thinking and preparedness has saved the city.

As the house lights come up the narrator notes: "You've observed the drama of self-defense."

Fort Wayne citizens deemed the film a success, and Commander Bowser encouraged representatives from the Office of Civil Defense in Washington, D.C., to buy the rights to the film and screen it elsewhere.

James Landis, the director of Civil Defense, congratulated Bowser on a "very excellent job" before informing him that they would not be purchasing the film but wished Fort Wayne and its movie the best of luck.

Q. What precautions can a person take and what can be used to combat an incendiary bomb?

A. Sand is the most efficient material which can be used to smother such a bomb. Water can be sprayed, but not poured in a steady stream on the bomb first to avoid the possibility of the fire spreading. Then the sand should be poured over the bomb until it is entirely covered. It can then be picked up in a shovel and placed in a partially filled bucket. A bucket with about six inches of sand in it will be satisfactory. The bucket can be carried out by using the handle of the shovel thrust through the handle of the bucket.

If I had been alive during the blackouts, I would have lived in District 5. My warden would have been Donald H. Jones of 3424 N. Washington Road. He would have called me the day prior to a blackout to remind me to close my blinds, extinguish all light, do my part to obliterate us from the aerial eyes of the Luftwaffe. He would have informed me not to strike a single match, and that if I needed to smoke—if I needed to calm my nerves—then I should have the courtesy to strike my light in a hallway far from the windows.

People still speak of the Civil Defense demonstration held in Hamilton Park so many years before. How the Civil Defense representative struck a single match from the outfield of the baseball diamond and how the citizens' faces erupted in firelight. How you could read the street sign: *Poinsette.*

Today, just a few hundred feet from that baseball diamond, a plaque reads "In honor of all who served in the armed forces of the Second World War from the Third Civilian Defense District."

I would have been in the fifth district. I have yet to find our plaque.

Q. To sum up the situation, what would you say would be most essential then for the protection of a home?

A. A hose of approximately 50 feet in length. A bucket, a long handled shovel and a supply of sand are the most essential requirements.

As other cities and manufacturers became aware of Fort Wayne's bombing problem, Fort Wayne mayor Harry Baals began receiving literature on the latest anti-bomb technology in order to safeguard the city from foreign attacks.

For just $2.50, one could purchase a Bomb-Quench.

"Bomb-Quench may be used with complete ease by anyone in home or factory" claims the brochure. "Simply remove top from the tube carton, sprinkle free flowing Bomb-Quench over the burning bomb or magnesium fire."

Or if Fort Wayne citizens preferred, they could invest in the Bomb-Snatcher, an orange metal scoop that stifled unexploded bombs.

"With the Bomb-Snatcher, removal of burning bombs is speedy and safe," the pamphlet promises.

However, the people of Fort Wayne were far more interested in simply buying bombs themselves. A dozen practice incendiary bombs could be purchased for just over seven dollars.

"Our Bomb is low in cost and its action similar to a real one," the pamphlet assures prospective buyers. "Dispel the fear which nearly all persons have of an Incendiary Bomb by giving them an opportunity to see these PRACTICE INCENDIARY BOMBS demonstrated and actually allowing them to practice with one."

Intrigued, Commander Bowser wrote the Baltimore Fire Works Company: "Will you please advice [sic] us if you have available for demonstration purposes any small incendiary bombs. Also, quote us prices, quantities and delivery date."

There is no evidence Fort Wayne ever purchased a bomb, nor is there evidence we ever experienced one.

A few years back, while driving along Jefferson Boulevard, I momentarily lost sight of the city's one and only skyscraper. Thankfully, it remained intact—just hidden in the fog.

Q. Do you feel that because of our inland location, the possibility of an air raid is very remote and that all these preparations are in vain?

A. I certainly do not want to say such a raid is impossible here, nor do I want to say that it is sure to come. I do however know that if we are raided these precautions and this training program will be invaluable. You don't carry fire insurance on your home because you are sure you will have a fire. You carry it for protection when it might be needed.

If you look hard enough in Lindenwood Cemetery, eventually you'll stumble across the gravestone of Victor F. Rea, the man responsible for creating the Rea Magnet Wire Company and bringing Hitler's name to every citizen's lips. If you look harder still, you'll find Ryan Woodward's grave as well, a slab of perfectly polished black marble, photos of him and his family laser-etched into the stone. Fourteen flags surround the monument, and even though the burial took place in 2007, at last glance there were still fresh roses resting their petaled heads against his name.

I wonder what room we were in at Lindley Elementary when Ryan and I first learned of Hitler, learned what a bomb was, what small arms were, wondering if we would ever die by them and if so, who would remember our names.

The day Truman announced the end of the war—August 14, 1945—the Fort Wayne newspapers were on strike. Airplanes buzzed over the city, though they did not drop bombs.

They dropped leaflets.

JAPAN SURRENDERS! TUNE INTO WGL FOR NEWS.

According to local newspapers, Fort Wayne's children crouched over the fallen materials and struggled to make out the words. When they finally did—sounding out every last syllable—the children ran up and down Bowser Avenue banging pots and pans, no longer fearing even fear itself.

On Calhoun Street, cars honked as bells rang from the spared church steeples, while not far away, the GE symbol re-lit the sky.

For the first time in a long time, Fort Wayne's newspaper's had good news to report

Q. If we were to be subjected to a bombing attack, what type bombs would probably be used against us?

A. We would first, in all probability, be bombed by Incendiary Bombs.

But we were not.

We were just prepared for it.

You, too, have observed the drama of self-defense.

The Year of the Great Forgetting

The fever strikes, and we, too, are struck by it, my wife and I suddenly jarred awake by the same cold sweat that's worked into Henry's small frame. In his eighteen months (541 days), this is the first of these sweats, and therefore the scariest. Mainly because it is without cause, an unexpected overture to an illness we can't yet see.

All of this takes place a thousand or so miles from our home, in a cabin in the woods in the Poconos. We'd found ourselves there at my mother's suggestion. "A nice halfway point," she'd argued, "so we can spend a little quality time together." I agreed to the trip, not because the Poconos were a halfway point by any measure, but because I'd recently endured an existential crisis brought on by the purchase of a minivan, and a road trip, I figured, might help me acclimate to my new life in the slow lane.

Once the decision was made, I immediately began poring over maps, a maniacal Magellan hell-bent on arranging a 2,800-mile road trip from Wisconsin to the east coast. As a result of my overzealousness, what began as a three-night stay in the Poconos quickly morphed into what we'd later call a "cross-your-legs-because-I'm-not-pulling-over" death march, complete with stops in Hartford, Salem, and Niagara Falls. We had no vested interest in any of these places, but I was lured by the open road.

We are the proud-ish owners of a minivan, I reminded myself. *Shouldn't we at least see what this baby can do?*

What that baby did was safely transport us to a resort in the Poconos, which I will politely describe as "rustic." Perhaps I am being polite even to call it a resort. The place was a shadow of its former grandeur, a towering farmhouse surrounded by paper-thin cabins, each in a unique state of disarray. We occupied one such cabin when Henry's cries burst through the night, stirring the surrounding wildlife, or at least my parents in the next cabin over.

Exhausted from the drive, I remained in my stupor throughout his first wave of wails, trapped in a half sleep that, for eighteen months, I'd persuaded myself was all the sleep I needed. Meanwhile, Meredith—for whom sleep has become a hypothetical—walks with her arms outstretched toward the crib, my zombie bride tripping over suitcases and still-wet swimsuits on her way to our burning boy.

She presses a hand to him, and he sizzles.

"He's hot," she whispers.

"How hot?" I ask.

"Hot-hot," she says. "*Scary* hot."

There they are again—the words that stir me awake. Suddenly I am groping for the thermometer, running my hands over countertops and patting the carpet. I frisk suitcases, unzip zippers in the dark, turn inside out every last sock on the off chance the thermometer is hiding.

The thermometer, apparently, is hiding. At least from me.

"So what now?" I ask. "Do we turn on the light?"

"Do you want him up for the next three hours?"

The tone of her voice indicates that we do not, so I try a new tack: relying on the glow of my cell phone screen to sweep the room for the thermometer.

"Just . . . forget it," Meredith shouts over his wailing. "Grab a wet washcloth, would you?"

Washcloth, I think, *washcloth, washcloth . . .*

I repeat the word all the way to the bathroom, then flick on the light, startling myself with my reflection.

Jesus! I think, staring hard at the sallow-faced creature staring back. *Aren't you supposed to be on vacation?*

But much like sleep, vacations, too, have become hypotheticals—another concept my wife and I once knew but now know better.

I turn the faucet and watch the washcloth bloom in my hands.

Meanwhile, just a wall away, Henry continues his ear-splitting vibrato. My blood pressure rises as he moves up the scale, until at last he hits a pitch I never knew possible. In that moment—as he holds his note—what I want most in the world is to take cover beneath the cool side of my pillow. But since I'm the father and this banshee is allegedly my son, I know my role is to provide protection, not take it.

Washcloth in hand, I bypass my pillow and start the walk toward his crib.

Why can't this be something simple? I wonder. *A bee sting or a bear attack? Something we know how to fix.*

103.1

The following morning, Meredith taps her hand to the glass of a Walgreens as the employee unlocks the door.

"Good morning," the employee says.

It isn't. Our boy is feverish, after all, and we are in need of a thermometer.

Meanwhile, in my own attempt to keep his body cool, Henry and I search for deer in the windblown field directly behind the cabin.

"We're looking for *deer*," I say, waiting for him to parrot it back.

"Deya," he says.

"Deer," I correct.

"Deya," he says again.

This goes on for quite some time.

My parents exit their own cabin, and suddenly half the resort knows of Henry's condition.

"He'll be fine," I assure every well-wishing stranger. "Just a fever, nothing more."

By the time Meredith returns, we have seen no deer, though I have undergone any number of religious conversions, promising everything but my firstborn in exchange for my firstborn. I cash in my karma, then pray to all the smiting gods that they might take their smiting elsewhere. I barter, I bargain, I beg. I swear off every last vice that I know.

As I carry Henry back into the cabin, as we insert the thermometer into his rectum, it becomes clear that my prayers have missed their mark.

Our hearts sink as the numbers continue to climb.

99 . . . 100 . . . 101 . . . 102 . . . 103.1 . . .

Henry laughs as the thermometer beeps, while Meredith and I look to one another.

And then, the afterthought amid all of this:

"Hey," I say, "happy five-year anniversary."

99.3

Suddenly, like an Old Testament miracle, our prayers are answered. By mid-afternoon the fever has broken, his temperature dropping to near normal. There is no explanation for the change. I have sacrificed no rams upon any altars. In fact, we have done nothing but wet washcloths and search for deer and hurl our prayers to the sky. Thankfully, one of the prayers seemed to have stuck, though it prompted a new fear: Which promise to God do I now need to make good on?

During Henry's afternoon nap we grow bold, Meredith and I charging my mother with babysitting duty while we slip off to a nearby waterfall we'd discovered in the woods.

The previous night, as I searched on hands and knees for the thermometer, I'd considered carrying Henry to those falls. At 3:00 AM it seemed logical, imperative even—no better way to break the fever than by drowning it in a stream. Thankfully, sounder minds prevailed, and rather than a nighttime hike down a ravine with my son, we made do with the washcloth instead.

Now Meredith and I take that walk without him, slipping down the slope until our sandals return to flat ground. I unpack

the wine and cheese and chocolate atop a mossy rock and we clink
plastic cups to our marriage.

"Let's make a wish," Meredith says, "for anything in the world."
We close our eyes, take a sip, and wish for 98.6.

99.5

Thanks to my white-knuckled driving (not to mention my high
tolerance for backseat screeching), we make it to every last stop
on the itinerary. In Hartford, Henry's screaming gets him kicked
out of the Mark Twain house ("A regular Huck Finn," I joke). He
fares better in Salem, where we remove ourselves on our own ac-
cord from the good ship *Friendship* docked in the harbor.

Henry's best behavior occurs in the place we need it least: at
the bottom of Niagara Falls, where thousands of gallons of roaring
water immediately lull him to sleep.

After surviving all of this, we pull back into the driveway,
where I promise myself to dedicate the rest of August to not going
anywhere. Twenty-eight hundred miles have left us weathered,
and though the minivan has performed admirably, we know it's
time to let that baby cool.

From here on out we walk, I proclaim, and for most of that
month we do.

Thankfully, we live just a few houses down from a playground,
which satisfies most of Henry's hierarchy of needs. And what
needs we can't fulfill in the sand, or on the slide, or in the swoop
of the swing, we find in the river instead. This, too, satisfies our
walking requirement. We regularly march our swimsuited bodies down the hidden path toward the river's inlet. It's a freshwater
paradise, a shaded glade once used to float timber into the river in
the days when timber still ruled this town. Now, all that remains

are the splintered pylons protruding like spikes from the sand, each of which Henry hugs while trying to keep from tumbling into the water.

Amid all this summertime fun I forget about his fever, and when it returns in mid-August—lingering for well over a week— we just continue our afternoon swims as if nothing has changed.

What this boy needs, I think, *is cool waters.*

It is a theory I'd nearly put to the test during our burning night in the Poconos. There, in that strange place with the waterfall so near, it had seemed the only logical choice.

And now, though we are closer to home, it still seems worth a try.

After all, if this fever refuses to reveal its source, what choice do we have but to exorcise it by equally mysterious means?

For weeks, I return Henry to the stream under the auspices of play.

"Shall we play?" I ask as I tug his trunks over his thighs. "Let's just go for a little play in the water."

"Wawa," he says.

"Water," I correct.

"Wawa," he says again.

99.5

Despite the stream's best efforts, we cannot break our boy's fever. Cannot even lower it a tenth of a point. Though his temperature is hardly extreme, it is nonetheless troubling—proof of some cog out of alignment.

I take to the phones, calling nurse after nurse like a seasoned telemarketer. I beg them for answers, and when none are given, I beg for a doctor instead.

Fine, a nurse finally relents. *We'll set something up.*

Upon our arrival at pediatrics later that day, the nurse begins with Henry's temperature. Henry's eyes roll across his brow as she sweeps a path across his forehead.

As the nurse peers down at the reading, I await confirmation that all my worry was reasonable, that I was right to advocate so fiercely on his behalf.

"Ninety-eight-point-six," she says, jotting the numbers down on her sheet. "Right this way for the doctor."

As a result of his perfect reading, the doctor has a hard time taking me seriously. He has seen parents like me before.

"Viral," he says. "It's probably just viral, and it'll pass."

I don't believe him. Don't believe the nurse, either.

They're in cahoots, I reason, part of some grand conspiracy to mislead parents into thinking their children healthy.

Though we have at last obtained our 98.6, I refuse to be satisfied. Mainly, because I know it can't be true. I convince myself that the fever has merely evolved, found a way to hold its hot breath until after the nurse's thermometer passed by.

You can trick them, I think as we pull into the Walgreens parking lot. *But you can't trick me.*

I return home with a new thermometer—top of the line—and insert it into my son.

Together, we wait for its beep just like always, and when it does—when Henry mimics the sound with which he's become so familiar—I glance the truth in the tiny screen.

How can it be? I wonder. *How is he already back to burning?*

I have no choice but to protect my son the only way I know how—by rigging the thermometer readings. I stick the probe halfheartedly beneath his arm and wait for the result.

"There. That's better," I smile as I read the screen. "A perfect 89.1."

All of this is lunacy, of course, but I am going mad. A part of me convinces the other part that there is logic in tricking the thermometer into giving me the reading I require. That same part of me dismisses my own powers of observation. It doesn't matter that Henry's acting the same and eating the same and playing the same—the thermometer counteracts everything I once knew to be true.

Prior to Henry's birth, a seasoned father warned me of the perils of fatherhood. He told me I would doubt myself and fail often, but that these transgressions were all par for the course. But then he offered a far more troubling thought: that although I would love every moment with my son, exhaustion would make certain that I hardly remembered any of it. At least not the first year, which he'd dubbed The Year of the Great Forgetting—a phrase I'm just beginning to understand.

Yet even now, midway through Henry's second year, my forgetfulness remains great. I can't help but feel as if the fever senses my weakness, pegs me for an easy mark by the crow's feet in the corners of my eyes.

Let me just sneak in a quick catnap, I think as my eyes droop toward my boy, *then I swear to God I'm coming for you.*

On Henry's 613th day of life we run the tests—all of them—anxious to learn the fever's name. We can't help but think that we know it, though we don't want what we think to be true.

On the doctor's orders, I lay Henry flat on the table and cover his body with my own.

"You're going to be fine," I say. "It'll all be over soon."

The lie is so real I believe it.

Henry has no reason to doubt me, so he grins, then begins babbling in a language I'll never know.

I steady him as the nurse readies the needle, then inserts it into his arm. The flesh of my flesh is broken, and for a moment, the babbling stops. Henry's body buckles, turns rigid, and then he lets loose, wailing as if trapped in the Mark Twain house or aboard a ship in Salem harbor.

The only word he knows to be of any use to him is no: "No, no, no, no, no, no, no, no, no."

"It's going to be fine, boy . . ."

"No, no, no, no, no, no, no, no, no."

I press down hard upon his body as the vials fill with blood.

With each rise in pitch, my body trembles.

I think: *Give me the ram, the altar, the sharpened knife. I am ready to make good on my promise.*

TEMPERATURE UNKNOWN

The tests come back, and since the doctors still don't know what it is, we settle for what it's not. It is not cancer, it is not Lyme disease, it is not anything we have a name for. Our pediatrician is pleased to inform us that the blood culture is negative for bacteria, that the white blood cell count looks good.

"So what is it?" I ask.

He says that's a little less clear.

When I ask what to make of the continual low-grade fever, he reminds me that temperatures fluctuate, that some children just run warm.

The easiest fix, we're told, is simply to lay off the thermometer for a while.

My jaw drops, though I soon admit this seems like sound advice.

Two months later, our boy is back to being a boy. Just some kid who will quickly forget what we will always remember.

Of all my parental trespasses, the one I'll never forget is how I placed my faith in numbers and not our son. How many afternoons had he hugged pylons in the stream to assure me he was fine? And how many times had I ignored him? Why was it easier for me to trust a beep and a screen than the person I loved most?

Some days I want to wear a button that reads IT'S MY FIRST DAY ON THE JOB. But I want to wear it always, because every day feels like the first day, and every lapse in judgment feels wholly my own.

Today is my 670th day on the job, though I am no better at it than I was yesterday. As proof, you need look no further than my forgetting to zip Henry's coat as we sit on the deck and watch the leaves fall alongside the outdoor thermometers. We grip the porch railing and peer into our backyard wilderness.

"Hey, boy," I say as we shiver, "how about you and I look for some deer?"

"Deya," he says.

"Deer," I correct.

"Deya," he says again.

I smile, pull him close, and save every last breath I've got for a moment he might remember.

Hirofukushima

Before there was nothing, there was everything: a flash like magnesium, followed by the darkness. By 1945, the people of Hiroshima had grown accustomed to the flashbulbs that preserved them in photographs, though they remained unfamiliar with the curious light they glimpsed in the sky one early August morning.

What, they wondered, *could possibly cause such a—*

Across the ocean, there were men who could measure destruction to the kiloton, men who had done it just three weeks prior, while hidden behind dark glasses. In the hours leading up to the test, scientists and soldiers gathered in New Mexico's desert and placed bets on their creation's destruction.

Will we incinerate the entire planet, they wondered, *or simply some small part of it?*

Sixty-six years later and seven hundred miles from Hiroshima, a high school buddy of mine—let's call him John—glances up at a squawking speaker in his classroom in Sendai.

The voice on the speaker tries to warn him of what's soon to come, but the warning comes too late.

Please prepare yourself for—

It is Friday, March 11, 2011. John doesn't yet know it, but Japan's most powerful earthquake in modern history has just struck the east side of the island, triggering a tsunami that is soon to swell the city's shoreline.

This is not John's first earthquake, but it's his first earthquake like this—a world-churning undulation that grinds his teeth to dust. The event itself is indescribable, even for John, who for years will struggle to find a language to match its power. All he will say is that the quake broke his frame of reference, forced him to rethink all he knew of rock and water.

Growing up in Indiana, John and I had never known disaster. Sure, we'd huddled alongside one another in our school's hallways in the midst of tornado drills, but they were always just that— drills—and thus the fear we felt was fake.

The real disaster came for him years later, in the form of an earthquake, a tsunami, and multiple partial nuclear meltdowns in the Fukushima Daiichi Nuclear Power Plant just fifty miles away.

This was no drill. The fear was not fake.

Let it end, John prays while clinging to the carpet, *please God, let it end.*

Fifteen-year-old Taeko Teramae glanced up from her place in the telephone office to spot a strange shape in the sky. She leaned toward a friend, but before she could speak the building crumpled around her—not an earthquake, but an eruption of another sort.

The kind that brought silence, followed by a dozen cries of *Mother!*

The school-age girls' accumulated voices rose up through the dust.

Mother! Mother!

A deafening roar followed by a deafening wail until their teacher, Mr. Wakita, told them to behave.

Taeko behaved, staying mostly mum as she freed herself from the rubble. She breathed, only to find that the world now smelled like the ash from Mount Aso.

Come, Mr. Wakita called to her, *can you swim across the river?*

She could so she did, following her teacher to the river, then into it, then to the safety on the other side.

She was reunited with her parents—*Mother! Father!*—both of whom lied to their daughter's broken face.

Your wounds are not serious, they assured her.

They knew nothing of radiation back then.

Once the shaking stops, John runs to his girlfriend—let's call her Hanako—and together, the pair retreats to their apartment. Hanako is native to Japan, an expert in earthquakes, and she, too, knows this one was different; that this was the kind that shakes snow from the sky as if shaking the leaves from the trees.

Suddenly, that snow is everywhere—a thick-flaked confetti drifting across John and Hanako's faces. For half an hour they huddle at their bus stop, but when the bus does not come they continue on foot.

The streets are cracked but quiet, nothing but the ceaseless sound of idling cars going nowhere. The sidewalks are mostly the same, and though small clusters of people pass one another, no one speaks to anyone.

This silence isn't out of the ordinary, nor is the sound of the idling cars. In fact, aside from the cracked window and crumbled walls, for the moment their world remains almost unchanged. The only indication that something is awry is the long line of people outside the convenience store, all of whom are anxious to buy their bento box of food.

John and Hanako don't need food; a six-month supply awaits them in their apartment. As they bypass the line, John is grateful for his foresight, glad to have thought of everything in advance.

It isn't until they enter their apartment to see the toppled water cooler flooding the floor that he learns a valuable lesson.

Only in retrospect, John thinks, *can you ever think of everything in advance.*

⚛

Look, a boy said, pointing out his classroom window, a B-29.

Thirteen-year-old Yoshitaka Kawamoto looked. Or attempted to look as he rose from his chair and headed toward the window.

Then, the blast, followed by the same wails Taeko heard in the telephone office:

Mother! Mother!

Yoshitaka woke to find himself trapped beneath debris.

Woke to the sound of familiar voices belting out the school song.

They sang to attract a rescue team, though eventually their dust-caked voices gave out. Yoshitaka's voice was the last to quit, though by the time it did, he'd freed himself from the rubble.

He became the rescue team, searching his shattered school for someone in need of saving.

Eventually he unearthed a classmate with a broken skull and a single eye but with breath still in his body.

Yoshitaka tried to save him but could not—the boy's lower half was buried deep.

The boy reached for a notebook in his chest pocket, cried *Mother! Mother!* as Yoshitaka retrieved it for him.

You want me to take this along to hand it over to your mother? Yoshitaka asked.

Mother! Mother! the boy replied.

Yoshitaka nodded, then burst through the smoke toward the playground, kicking at the hands that reached for his ankles.

What he needed was water—something to clear his throat—so he ran toward the Miyuki Bridge over the Kyobashi River. But when he arrived at its bank, he learned that the river was clotted with dead people.

Still, he drank deeply as a mushroom cloud blossomed overhead.

He knew nothing of radiation back then.

John and Hanako marvel at the wreckage inside their apartment, amazed at how everything has found its wrong place.

Here are the books and here is the water, they think, *but why are they together?*

Tiptoeing over the soggy pages, they make their way to the fridge. The earthquake has rendered them powerless, and though they risk spoiling the food, they open the fridge door all the same.

Inside, they find an inordinate supply of milk, cream, and blueberries, and since they cannot yet wrap their heads around what has occurred—or what is occurring inside reactor 1 at the Fukushima plant—they whip the cream and dip the berries and feast amid destruction.

It is not a last meal. Why would it be?

They knew nothing of radiation back—

Eiko Taoka and her one-year-old son rode the streetcar in search of a wagon. Their apartment building was soon to be evacuated, and a wagon was needed to assist in their move.

As the streetcar neared the station, Eiko's arms began to grow weak. She'd been holding her son for quite some time, and as she adjusted him in her arms, she caught the attention of the woman seated directly in front of her.

I will be getting off here, the woman said. *Please take this seat.*

Eiko thanked the woman, but as she and her son prepared to sit she noticed a strange smell, a strange sound, and then darkness.

Eiko's one-year-old son was staring out the window when the glass blasted from the streetcar. His face shattered, but even then he turned to his mother and smiled.

In the three weeks he had left to live, Eiko gave her son what comfort she could, offering him her breast and allowing him to suckle everything she had inside her.

The radiation, too.

John and Hanako try to sleep, but eventually they just stop trying. They have lost their faith in the earth. The aftershocks continue throughout the first night, though what scares them most isn't the possibility of another major quake, but what even a tremor might do to the already compromised structure of their apartment.

Their hearts flutter with every shift of the bedsheets.

I should have seen it coming, John thinks as he lies in bed. *There were just so many signs.*

He means literal signs. Signs on buses and streets and the sides of buildings—all of them warning of the long-overdue earthquake soon to strike Sendai. Over time, these signs had become so ubiquitous that even John of Indiana knew better than to believe them.

A few nights before The Earthquake struck, another earthquake struck. It didn't cause John to grind his teeth to dust, but it did stir him awake.

He sat up, turned to Hanako, whispered, *What if this is the foreshock?*

⚛

Senkichi Awaya, mayor of Hiroshima, sat down to his morning breakfast. His thirteen-year-old son, as well as his two-year-old granddaughter, joined him.

Perhaps he quartered an orange for young Ayako, poured Shinobu a cup of tea.

Sweetheart, perhaps he said, *be careful not to spill the—*

The clink of a teacup, followed by a fireball.

Sweetheart!

That afternoon, when the mayor could not be reached, the city treasurer sifted through the wreckage of the mayoral residence and found Senkichi's scorched skeleton inside.

His reign was over. The radiation was not.

On Saturday morning John and Hanako wake to find their world has not yet changed.

Yes, they are still without power, but otherwise, it is a normal Saturday morning following an earthquake.

They leave their apartment and search the row of nearby shops for an outlet to charge a phone. What they find instead are swarms of people with similar plans, gripping their phones and waiting for the outlets.

Guess we're out of luck, John thinks, though as they return to their apartment, Hanako spots a beacon—a glowing traffic light—just beyond their home.

Could it be? they wonder. *Is it back?*

They bustle up the stairs, swing wide the door, and find their luck has changed.

The power is back, which means their lives are back as well. They have running water, internet, and more food than they can eat.

Their good fortune is enough to keep them in Sendai while others flee.

We are safe here, they think, while fifty miles away the core of a reactor melts.

Ten days after the blast that killed her father, brother, and child, Motoko Sakama—the mayor's daughter—boarded a train to see what remained of her father's city. When she stepped from the train, she found that what little remained was all but unrecognizable.

Motoko walked for miles, until at last reaching the home where her injured mother lay.

I am so sorry, her mother said, *for the death of Ayako.*

Motoko's mother explained how Senkichi, Shinobu, and Ayako had just finished breakfast as the air-raid warning lifted.

How, for a moment, everyone felt fine.

Initially, when Motoko's father's and brother's skeletons were recovered, her young daughter was nowhere to be found. But upon closer inspection, once the ash was swept clean, the two-year-old's skeleton was unearthed alongside Senkichi's.

The grieving Motoko was left to draw but a single conclusion: *My father held my daughter as their bodies burned away.*

For a moment, everyone felt—

By Sunday evening their world has begun to change. John and Hanako have heard rumors of problems at the Fukushima plant, and though they are just rumors, they are enough to give John pause.

In a search bar, he types: HOW TO SURVIVE FALLOUT.

John's internet search yields more than he ever wanted to know. Suddenly he knows its language: *radiation, contamination, alpha, gamma, beta.*

John and Hanako discuss the possibility of leaving. Of flagging a taxi, or renting a car, or purchasing plane tickets. The problem, though, is that the taxis are low on gas, the rental cars rented, and thus, even with plane tickets in hand, there is no way to reach the airport.

Add to this the unspeakable problem of radiation: the knowledge that every time you open a door there's no telling what might slip inside.

John stares at the vents, the windows, the doorway, and thinks: *Every crack is a killer.*

He wants to tape the cracks shut, as one website suggested, and though he has no tape, he knows where he can find some.

He pulls on a sweatshirt, a surgical mask, waves goodbye, and walks out the door.

Then, he steps back into his city (which is dead), and the streets (which are empty), and tries to reorient himself in a place that once felt like home.

But his home is now populated with ghosts, the buildings are ghosts, and each window in each building is just another entry point for the radiation to make more ghosts.

John turns a circle, thinks of the bustle of the people on that street the week before. Thinks how before it took to trembling, the world was something else—something it would never be again.

Still, some parts remain unchanged. Like the office building just a few blocks away, which he enters, heading toward a supply closet he'd noticed in passing months prior.

There is no one anywhere, so he helps himself to the tape.

He helps himself by helping himself to the tape.

Weeks before the blast, a young student left Hiroshima to enjoy his summer break among family. He was the sumo wrestling champion of his small town, and he enjoyed his hero's welcome.

As the break came to its end, the young man's friends took the train back to school, though the young man decided to stay home for one day more.

A bomb dropped in the time between, and the young man became one of the few young men of his class to survive.

Like Motoko, he, too, got off the train to find a landscape mostly stripped of landmarks.

And he, too, walked the crumbled streets trying to remember what was once where.

He walked until he discovered a metallic taste in his mouth.

Odd, he thought, and in an attempt to purge himself of the taste he took a drink of water. (He knew nothing of radiation back then.)

The young man grew sick, and soon his sumo wrestling days were over.

He could not fight two things at once.

The young man grew up, grew older, and though he and his wife were desperate for a child, after years with no luck they began to wonder if his exposure had made it impossible for them to conceive.

It had not.

In fact, one day many years later, even the young man's daughter would have a daughter—who we call Hanako—and sixty-six years later, she and John will sit in their apartment and know his fear firsthand.

It is not metal they taste that night, but blueberries and cream.

It is not the family's first nuclear incident, but their second.

Two and a half years after the Fukushima Daiichi nuclear disaster, John and I meet up for a beer.

Sitting cross-legged on my parents' couch, he tells me about the earthquake, the aftermath, and his decision to open the apartment door in an effort to retrieve the tape.

Was it worth it? I ask. Did you do the right thing when you opened the door?

John pauses, picks at the beer label.

Were you in Mr. Kuelling's senior seminar class? he asks.

I shake my head no.

John describes how the teacher assigned them to read Don DeLillo's *White Noise*, and how even as a high schooler, John had been troubled by a particular scene in the book; one in which a toxic chemical cloud drifts toward the main character and his family as the character stops to fill up for gas.

When I first read that book, I remember thinking, "Why doesn't he get back in his car while the gas pumps?" John says. "Why does he just stand out there breathing in the toxins?" But then, after the radiation started spreading throughout Sendai, suddenly I got it. I understood why the guy doesn't get back in the car.

Why? I ask. Why does a guy stay outside in a chemical cloud?

Because, John says, when you love your family, you don't open the door—you never open the door—unless you're going to get some tape.

On that August morning, thirty-three-year-old Isao Kita kept his eyes fixed on the sky. As the chief weatherman in the Hiroshima District, it was his job to do so. Isao cocked his head at a sound, then watched as a blinding flash far brighter than the sun erupted directly before him.

Glass broke, heat entered, and Isao winced as the smoke cut his city in half.

Though it was his job to understand the weather, he didn't know what to make of the strange black rain that followed.

He could hardly believe the way that rain stuck to every limb and every leaf it touched. Stuck to every body—every hand and foot and face left unprotected.

The rain marked the people and the place, and Isao, the chief weatherman of Hiroshima that morning, took note.

It couldn't be washed off, he later remarked. *I couldn't be washed off.*

On the Wednesday following the earthquake, John finds an unread message in his inbox.

According to a friend, beginning at dawn, one bus every hour is rumored to arrive from Yamagata.

Perhaps this might be your way out? the friend suggests.

That night, John and Hanako don't sleep. Instead, they decide how best to fit their lives into a suitcase. There is no room for sentimentality; all they take is a hard drive and dried fruit.

They zip their suitcase, lock their door, then start off toward the station.

It is 3:00 AM and raining, and though the rain is not black, John wonders: *What exactly is acid rain?*

They huddle beneath the bus station awning for hours, though even there they can't dodge the droplets that splatter sideways against their skin. Their breaths are shallow beneath their surgical masks, which make them feel safe.

Less is more, John thinks as he breathes. *Less is more.*

They distract themselves by watching the line grow behind them, and then—far more troubling—grow ahead of them as well.

People are cutting, John realizes. *They're stealing our seats and our lives.*

He considers confronting them but doesn't.

No one confronts anyone.

Although the lines are long and the buses are few, nobody says a thing.

They simply clutch their umbrellas and wait for the line to move forward.

When the first bus arrives at 6:00 AM, John and Hanako fill the last two seats.

Dr. Kaoru Shima—the proprietor of Shima Hospital—was assisting a colleague in nearby Mikawa when he learned of his city's destruction.

He was spared, though his hospital wasn't.

In fact, Shima Hospital was ground zero; the bomb had transformed the two-story structure to ruins, turned the bones of his patients to dust.

On the evening of August 6, Dr. Shima returned to Hiroshima, stood alongside the busted Chamber of Commerce building, and shouted to the survivors.

The director of Shima Hospital is here! he cried triumphantly. *Take courage!*

He knew nothing of anything then.

By day's end, John and Hanako step off a train platform in Akita, a city 150 miles northwest of Sendai.

Their flight to Tokyo isn't scheduled until the following day, so they wander the city, staring at a world seemingly unchanged. Everywhere, people are shopping, clutching their bags with one hand while holding their phones with the other.

People smile, people laugh, people snap selfies on the street. None of their cameras are out of batteries.

Have you not heard of Fukushima? John wants to scream at every passerby. *Or a city called Sendai?*

Dumbfounded, John and Hanako slide into a booth at a family restaurant and pretend they are a part of this unchanged world. They mull over the menu, studying their many options.

Within minutes, the waiter arrives to take their order.

They are famished and they are alive so they want everything.

Pizza, pasta, chocolate cake.

Make that two slices of cake, John says.

When the pizza arrives, John notices distress on the waiter's face.

I'm so sorry, the waiter says, *but the kitchen informs me that we have run out of fresh basil. There was an earthquake—perhaps you have heard?—and the trucks were unable to make the trip.*

John stares down at his feast while the poor man says, *Please, sir, will you accept my apologies?*

Dr. Shima set up his makeshift hospital at the primary school near the center of town. There, he did what he could, but as the bodies piled high, Dr. Shima realized he needed a way to dispose of the dead in order to make way for the living.

He ordered that a crematorium be built on the school's playground, and there for days the bodies of his townspeople burned.

Day and night one could smell the odor of burning flesh and watch the flickering fire of the funeral pyre, the doctor later recalled.

This time, fire was the cure, and though Dr. Shima treated the cuts and broken bones, he knew nothing of the purple spots that began dappling people's skin.

Radiation, he'd later learn. *The word is radiation.*

Upon deplaning in Seattle the following day, John finds that still the world has not changed.

It is the same America he always knew—complete with seven-dollar bagels and five-dollar coffees and a surplus of television screens.

From a TV in the terminal, he watches as Charlie Sheen speaks of tiger blood.

Have you not heard of Fukushima? John wonders as he stares at the screen. *Or a city called Sendai?*

Hanako pulls him to the baggage claim, where they soon hear a swarm of well-wishers cheer the safe arrival of a mother and father and their teenage son. The trio grins at their compatriots, making a grand display of pumping fists and flexing muscles while pointing to their matching T-shirts.

John glances their T-shirts and is surprised to see an outline of Japan and a red dot near his city.

The T-shirts read: I SURVIVED EARTHQUAKE 9.0!

More hooting, more hollering, more high fives than John can handle.

A TV bleats: *Actor Charlie Sheen claims that he has tiger blood...*

Come on, John says. *We need to get out of here.*

One summer evening many years back, a friend and I obliterated every last ant on the planet. At least it felt that way. We were seven, and on that moon-drenched night, we found a field behind our houses and turned its anthills to dust. Soon, that field would be a neighborhood anyway, but before the steamrollers rolled in we flattened the land by hand, told ourselves we were sparing them a worse fate.

As John and I sit in my parents' living room drinking our beers, we refrain from speaking of those men in the New Mexico desert. We don't talk about ants either, or whisper the names of the people who perished so long ago. In fact, we don't talk about the old disaster at all, just the one that is still ongoing.

People won't really know how bad it is for years, John says. *Not until the uptick in cancer, and the birth defects, and the shrinking attention spans. We won't know just like we didn't know with Chernobyl.*

What about your health? I ask. *Yours and Hanako's?*

We won't know either, he says.

In that moment on the couch, I might've said any number of things, but I don't say any of them.

Instead, I watch as John's eyes glaze over as he studies his beer bottle.

After a moment, he returns to me, clear-eyed, and tries to give me the old smile.

But enough about me, he says, delivering his line. *Tell me, what's new with you?*

Punch Line

One night when my wife is pregnant with our second child, she asks me for a glass of water. It's late, and though it is a minor request, I still grumble as I sleepwalk to the kitchen. Who can say what time it is? Even the clocks are asleep. But the water is there, and the glasses are there, and so I fill a glass to the brim. This is no hyperbole; I literally fill a glass to the brim, measure each droplet until the water forms a perfect plane. This is my idea of a joke.

My wife and I are exhausted—mostly the result of Henry's sleeping proclivities (i.e., not sleeping)—and so, we work in laughter wherever we can.

"Here," I say, straight-faced. "I've come bearing water."

"Why do you insist on doing this?" she asks, eyeing the brim.

(The last time she asked for a glass of water, I brought her a pitcher instead.)

"You're welcome," I say as she lifts herself up and chugs. "The pleasure's mine."

And then I feel another joke brewing—this one even better than the first.

I open my mouth but choke on my own laughter.

"What?" she asks, placing the glass alongside the fetal Doppler on the bedside table. "What's so funny?"

I shake my head; hold up a finger.

"What?"

I restart; compose myself by sliding a hand down my face.

"Now that . . ." I snort, "that there's . . ."

"That there's what? Seriously, why are you laughing?"

"Now that there's some good . . ."—I pause for the punch line—". . . water."

Maybe you have to be there to get it. Maybe you have to be us.

And maybe you have to know that the part that isn't funny (assuming there's a part here that is) is that I can count on one hand the number of times she's asked anything of me.

My slaphappy spreads, and soon she, too, is laughing.

"Quiet," she hisses, nodding toward our finally sleeping boy one room over. "You'll wake him."

"But that there water . . ." I say, wiping tears, ". . . that there was some good water, huh?"

"That's not funny," she says, but by then we're laughing so hard she's beginning to wonder if maybe it is.

Maybe this *is* funny, and maybe Henry's low-grade fever is funny, too. Maybe exhaustion is funny, and hiding heartbeats are funny, and every fear we'll ever face is just some form of funny.

"Oh, the lunacy of water, am I right?"

"Stop talking!" she repeats. "You're seriously going to wake him."

"Or her," I laugh, pointing to my wife's belly. "Maybe I'll wake her, too!"

The joke stops because my loose lips have made her real, turned our prophecy into a promise. We'd found her heartbeat just an hour before, and I'd grown bold, said a thing when I shouldn't have said a thing—made a her out of an almost her.

"Come on," my wife says. "Just shut up and come to bed."

I do both of these things.

But within a few hours I wake to the pitter-patter of my wife's feet en route to the bathroom.

I shoot up, anxious for some assurance that we are all still okay. That no signal has been dropped, no wires crossed, no message miscommunicated.

Then: the rumble of a toilet paper roll, a flush, and the return of the pitter-patter.

"Drink too much water?" I ask.

"She just loves punching me in the bladder," my wife groans, collapsing onto the bed. "It's like her favorite thing in the world."

I press my hand to the belly and close my eyes.

Good one, sweetheart, I think.

Bedtime Story

April 2014

Dear Daughter,

Once upon a time many years back, the citizens of Eau Claire, Wisconsin—your future home—tilted their heads skyward and observed what they couldn't explain. This was in 1870, back when lumberjacks still ruled the land and lived among the trees.

But on this particular night all their axe blades stopped swinging long enough to take in the unusual sight: a light that resembled the northern lights but was no northern light. Not only did it inhabit the wrong section of sky, but its movements were unlike anything the region had seen. It was a core of light expanding like a halo, soon joined by a second halo, both of which merged to form a pair of magician's rings in the sky.

I suppose the details don't much matter, dear. What matters is that the event was so mysterious that even the most grizzled lumberjacks were roused from their bunkhouses, forced to admit that even they—who'd seen it all—had never seen anything like that.

As the sawdust began settling like snow, those lumberjacks crossed their arms, fidgeted, and ran blistered fingers through bushy beards to try to make sense of the message being sent.

But what is the message? they wondered. *And who is sending it?*

I've asked similar questions of you, dear, trying hard to decipher your message through the static of the ultrasound. But the signal always drops—your image never budges—and some part of you continually remains unknown.

And what are we to make of that strange light in the sky? Well, it was different things to different people—a miracle, a mystery, a meteorological phenomenon. But it was the latter-most phrase that made it into the headline, a scientific catchall for the mostly indescribable event.

However, the newspaper correspondent—whose job it was to describe—much preferred depicting that light as a mystery, revealing the way it spread slowly "like the moonlight coming through a cloud, or the reflection of a prairie fire, putting out the stars nearest to it."

I've read the article a dozen times, and still I shudder at the splendor of the language; how it helps me see what I was not there to see, helps me know what I could not know.

I mention this because you are your own mystery, dear, and your message has only been half received. Which is why the doctors requested the second ultrasound, then the third, in the hope that we might get to know you better. Might untangle the wires, too, that have turned you to static on the screen; allow us to form a shape from your shadow.

A few days back your mother, brother, and I saw another shape—a wild turkey—that I immediately read as a sign. A sign that assured me that you are all right, that we are all right, that we will all be all right together.

It was Easter morning, and as your future family roamed the same woods those lumberjacks once roamed, the turkey in question clucked across our path.

I identified it as such—"Holy crap, a turkey!"—though in the three seconds between my voice and your family's reaction, the alleged turkey had already disappeared.

Your two-year-old brother—his name is Henry, you'll like him—turned to me with his toothy grin and tried to get the joke.

"You crazy, Dada," he laughed. "You crazy."

I am not crazy. I believed what I'd seen. And what I'd seen, I believed, was real.

But enough about turkeys; let us return our attention to the bedtime story about people who lift their heads to the sky. I want to teach you to marvel at that which you can't understand.

Once upon a time, in July of 1860, while so many remained asleep in their beds, a landscape painter named Frederic Edwin Church propped his head up on his pillow to peer up at the sky. He was honeymooning in the Hudson Valley (I'll explain when you're older), though once the meteor procession began, he couldn't help but reach for his sketchbook.

Love lasts a lifetime, he probably thought, *but meteors do not.*

And so that man sketched us the sky that night, tracing every trajectory so that we of the future might see what he saw in the past. Someday, dear, I'll show you his painting. We'll marvel at what we missed together.

But keep this in mind, also: sometimes what we miss can be good. Just ask Ann Elizabeth Hodges of Sylacauga, Alabama, who once upon a time was awakened by a meteorite that struck her in the hip.

Who can say how long it took for that meteorite to find her? To travel millions of miles—unbuckling itself from its asteroid belt—before hurtling through her roof. Who can say what convergence of events allowed for their collision, granting that poor woman the honor of being the first documented case of a human struck by a meteorite?

Which makes her what exactly? Lucky? Unlucky? Or just a woman who could not avoid what the universe had in store for her.

Here's a bit of advice, dear: the universe always has something in store for us. Sometimes it's a mysterious light; sometimes it's a wild turkey. And sometimes it's a collision of another sort, like the nursing student who, once upon a time a few weeks back, halted me in the student union.

"Excuse me," she said, "but are you interested in saving a life?"

Suddenly I was rubbing a cotton-tipped swab along my upper gum line.

"Like this?" I asked, and she assured me I was doing great. So great, in fact, that she handed me a second swab, then a third, and finally, after swabbing all four corners of my mouth, she gathered my DNA into the test kit and thanked me for placing myself on the bone marrow donor list.

"Sure," I said. "It was nothing."

And it was nothing, especially if it might help save somebody's son, somebody's daughter, somebody's somebody in need.

Which is mostly why I did it. Because I wanted to help somebody in the hopes that one day somebody might help me. That, and I felt embarrassingly guilty for all the marrow I had sloshing about in my bones. As I rubbed those swabs in my mouth—locked eyes with that nursing student—the only person I saw staring back at me was you.

Who, I wondered, *would dare leave life to luck if he might leave it to karma, instead?*

And these days, dear, we needn't leave anything to luck. Now we have ultrasounds, Dopplers, and DNA tests. We have tea leaves and divining rods. If we have a question about anything—landscape painting or the trajectories of meteorites—probably some app will assist us in finding our answer.

For better or worse, we live in a world mostly without mysteries (you are the exception). But we didn't always, and once upon a time even predicting something as simple as rain was somehow beyond our powers.

At least until a man named Léon Philippe Teisserenc de Bort decided he'd had quite enough of feeling powerless. After decades of disasters from the sky, this man began launching weather balloons, measuring wind speeds and velocities in the hope of providing accurate weather predictions for the benefit of us all.

Surely science can deduce the sky's mysteries, the balloon man reasoned; *surely science is the gospel truth.*

But he knew it was a false gospel unless scientists were willing to work together, to take their world and shrink it.

And so they did, constricting the world in something called telegraph wire, using codes and clicks to warn others of the weather soon to come.

In July of 1907—nearly forty years after those lumberjacks rubbed their bushy beards—the balloon man put his theory to the test, joining dozens of others across the world in a synchronized weather experiment. Kites flew in Hyde Park and Hamburg, in Strasburg, Simia, and beyond.

From over twenty locations, these men pinpricked the sky, watched as their kites crisscrossed in the crosswinds like telegraph wire, lassoing the mysteries from above.

But of course they couldn't lasso all of them. Rest assured, there are still mysteries in need of unraveling.

Like you, dear—your own mystery—and what are we to make of you, we who made you with the best materials we had?

It wasn't until midway through Mommy's pregnancy that the doctors grew concerned by that which we did not know. Not terribly concerned, mind you, but concerned enough to ask for the additional ultrasound; and then, later, the additional-additional ultrasound.

Just to be sure, they said.

Sure of what? we asked.

That everything is as it should be.

Since my body is useless in helping Mommy's body build your body, I tried offering myself to the universe, instead.

Crack me wide, suck my marrow; take whatever it is you need.

But I suppose there are always things we can't control—not even with our marrow.

After wasting a rainy afternoon in the grocery store, I buckled your brother into his seat as a young woman in a neon vest approached.

"Excuse me," she said, "but do you happen to be the owner of this minivan?"

149

My first instinct was to lie to her. To take a step back, give it a good hard look, and say, "You know, maybe this isn't my van . . ."

I had the sneaking suspicion, dear, that whatever she had to tell me wasn't good.

Perhaps I'd parked in a handicapped spot.

Or perhaps she had news about you, had managed to translate a message beyond the mumbles of medical science.

I nodded to her—"This is my van," I said—and she opened her mouth to speak.

"I'm sorry to have to tell you this . . ."

Dear God . . .

". . . but one of the carts left a dent on the back of your van. I was pushing the carts and I left the dent—"

Thank God . . .

The young girl was college-age or close, freckled, wearing a headband that held every drenched hair in place.

She escorted me to the back fender, holding her head low.

"I'm sorry."

The mark was all but unnoticeable, not even a dent, just a scratch.

I assured her it was fine. That we would be fine.

"Are you sure?" she asked. "Because you can tell someone."

"Don't worry," I repeated. "If you hadn't told me, I wouldn't have even known."

I waved, drove away, and in the rearview, caught a glimpse of her rain-dappled face.

She is somebody's daughter, I thought.

Which is what I often think now when things go awry, when composition papers flutter in late or additional dings are added to the minivan. I remind myself that every woman is somebody's daughter, dear, and every man is somebody's son.

And because of this—because everybody surely cares for somebody, or should—we should all care about probabilities as well.

What's a probability, you ask?

It's a way for grown-ups like Daddy to sleep easier at night, particularly when the numbers assure us that bad things will always affect somebody else. We needn't fear meteorites, for example, when we know the low odds of getting struck.

Then again, every time we speak of one-in-a-million odds, we should always consider the one, the Ann Elizabeth Hodges, who was minding her own business when the universe conspired against her. When she and a meteorite reminded the world that the crisis is always averted until it isn't, that *what ifs* are always just that until they aren't.

The night before your final ultrasound, I ask the universe to conspire with me instead. I scan the skies for clues, but the stars remain mum, offering me little to go on.

Following a restless night I wake early, and suddenly, the signs are everywhere: in the fog of the bathroom mirror, in the oil stain in the garage.

There are too many signs, and so I shut out the world and open a book instead.

I am trying to read my way out of disaster, I am trying to read my way out of disaster . . .

But I've hardly cracked the spine of *To Kill a Mockingbird* before I find myself resorting to bibliomancy, stabbing at the sentences, desperate for one last clue.

And finally, the clue emerges and clears up all that static.

There, at the tip of my index finger, I read the words like tarot cards:

"You're a strong girl . . ."

And suddenly I believe that you are; I can feel it in my marrow.

Listen carefully now, because this is the last story I'll tell you, dear, before you wake to this world.

Once upon a time a daddy believed that a mysterious light was more than a mysterious light, that a meteor was more than a meteor. He believed in probabilities and prophecies, in wild turkeys and girls wearing headbands in the rain. He believed in the power and the glory of a quartet of cotton swabs, believed he'd glimpsed the future in a minivan bumper.

Dear, you would never believe all the silly things this silly daddy believed.

But he was not crazy because he believed what he'd seen. And what he'd seen, he believed, was you.

WORKS CONSULTED

Here is a selected list of works consulted and utilized throughout the included essays.

BEDTIME STORY

Hall, John. *The Day the Meteorite Fell in Sylacauga.* September 14, 2010. http://issuu.com/randymecredy /docs/_hodges_amnh_pdf_9-2010/1?e=2079579/4002986.

New York Times. "Kites Are to Fly All Over the World." July 15, 1907, 6.

———. "Meteorological Phenomenon in Wisconsin." January 16, 1870, 1.

———. "To Predict Weather Months Ahead." August 8, 1909, 1.

DEATH BY REFRIGERATOR

Adams, Cecil. "Is It Impossible to Open a Refrigerator Door from the Inside?" *The Straight Dope.* March 4, 2005. http:// www.straightdope.com/columns/read/2586/is-it-impossible -to-open-a-refrigerator-door-from-the-inside.

Association of Home Appliance Manufacturers. "Chest Freezer Safety Brochure." Accessed April 1, 2015. http://www.aham .org/ht/a/GetDocumentAction/i/586.

Campbell, Robert Jean. *Campbell's Psychiatric Dictionary.* Oxford: Oxford University Press, 2009.

Dubuque Telegraph-Herald. "Refrigerator Death Traps." Advertisement. July 4, 1976.

Fodor, Nandor. *The Search for the Beloved: A Clinical Investigation of the Trauma of Birth and Pre-Natal Conditioning.* New York: Hermitage Press, 1949.

Karp, Harvey. *The Happiest Baby on the Block: The New Way to Calm Crying and Help Your Baby Sleep Longer.* New York: Bantam, 2002.

Kraus, Jeff. "Effectiveness of Measures to Prevent Unintentional Deaths of Infants and Children from Suffocation and Strangulation." *Public Health Reports* 100, no. 2 (March–April 1985): 231–240.

Lan, Russell. "Refrigerator Death Trap for 3 Children." *Meridian Journal.* August 12, 1964.

Ludington Daily News. "G.R. Man Is Arraigned in Refrigerator Deaths." July 29, 1987, 1.

Öst, Lars-Göran. "The Claustrophobia Scale: A Psychometric Evaluation." *Behaviour Research & Therapy* 45, no. 5 (2007): 1053–1064.

Sarasota Herald-Tribune. "Refrigerator Death Declared Accident." July 15, 1967, 10.

Toledo Blade. "Junk Refrigerator Death Trap for 2." June 2, 1954, 2.

Wikipedia. S.v. "Oliver Evans." Last modified December 17, 2014.

DISPATCHES FROM THE DROWNINGS

Archimedes. "On Floating Bodies." *The Works of Archimedes.* Edited by Thomas L. Heath. Cambridge: Cambridge University Press, 1897.

Bierens, Joost J. L. M., ed. *Handbook on Drowning: Prevention, Rescue, Treatment.* Berlin: Springer, 2006.

Centers for Disease Control and Prevention. "Drowning
   Happens Quickly: Learn How to Reduce Your Risk." May
   2012. http://www.cdc.gov/Features/drowningprevention/.
Drowning: Historical, Statistical Methods of Resuscitation. Boston:
   Lungmotor Company, 1920.
Holy Bible. King James Version. New York: American Bible
   Society, 1999.
Johnson, I. D. *A Guide to Homeopathic Practice; Designed for the
   Use of Families and Private Individuals.* New York: Boericke &
   Tafel, 1892.
1911 Class Encyclopedia. S.v. "Drowning and Life Saving." 11th ed.
   1911. http://en.wikisource.org/wiki/1911_Encyclop%C3
   %A6dia_Britannica/Drowning_and_Life_Saving.
Oxford Dictionaries. S.v. "Holocaust," def. 1.
Trelawny, Edward. *Recollections of the Last Days of Shelley and
   Byron.* Boston: Ticknor and Fields, 1858.
Wikipedia. S.v. "Drownings at Nantes." Last modified October
   11, 2014.

EPISTLE TO AN EMBRYO

Bishop, Elizabeth. *The Complete Poems, 1927–1979.* New York:
   Farrar, Straus and Giroux, 1983.

FIFTY WAYS OF LOOKING AT TORNADOES

Bernard-Donals, Michael. "The Rhetoric of Disaster and the
   Imperative of Writing." *Rhetoric Society Quarterly* 31, no. 1
   (2001): 73–94.
Branley, Franklyn Mansfield, and Leonard P. Kessler. *Tornado
   Warning: A Booklet for Boys and Girls.* Washington, D.C.:
   U.S. Department of Commerce, National Oceanic and
   Atmospheric Administration, 1981.

Cobb, Mark, and Katherine Lee. "Shelters, Clinics Take In Displaced Pets." *Tuscaloosa News,* May 1, 2011, 11A.

Condra, G. E., and G. A. Loveland. "The Iowa-Nebraska Tornadoes of Easter Sunday, 1913." *Bulletin of the American Geographical Society* 46, no. 2 (1914): 100–107.

Copley, John T. "The Movements and Forces in Tornadoes." *Transactions of the Kansas Academy of Science* 38 (1935): 213–215.

Holden, Edward S. "A System of Local Warnings against Tornadoes." *Science* 2, no. 37 (1883): 521–522.

Landsberg, H. E. "Psychological Responses to Tornadoes." *Science* 180, no. 4086 (1973): 544, 546, 588.

Leighly, John. "An Early Drawing and Description of a Tornado." *Isis* 65, no. 4 (1974): 474–486.

Lemons, Hoyt. "Physical Characteristics of Disasters: Historical and Statistical Review." *Annals of the American Academy of Political and Social Science* 309 (1957): 1–14.

Macfarlane, James. "Evidence of Unrecorded Tornadoes." *Science* 3, no. 59 (1884): 346–347.

Montgomery (Alabama) Advertiser. "Rescuers Find Baby All Alone in Cotton Field." March 23, 1932.

Science. "Tornadoes, and How to Escape Them." Vol. 4, no. 99 (1884): 572–573.

Science News. "Tornadoes, a Mystery." Vol. 91, no. 18 (1967): 422–424.

Science News-Letter. "Monopoly on Tornadoes Held by America." Vol. 5, no. 171 (1924): 10.

———. "Tornadoes Made in Laboratory Box." Vol. 68, no. 10 (1955): 147.

Sims, John H., and Duane D. Baumann. "The Tornado Threat: Coping Styles of the North and South." *Science* 176, no. 4032 (1972): 1386–1392.

Talman, C. F. "Most Tornadoes Do Little Damage." *Science News-Letter* 11, no. 315 (1927): 261.

Tuscaloosa News. "Obama: I've Never Seen Destruction Like This." April 30, 2011, 1.

Vonnegut, B., and James R. Weyer. "Luminous Phenomena in Nocturnal Tornadoes." *Science* 153, no. 3741 (1966): 1213–1220.

Wikipedia. S.v. "John Parker Finley." June 23, 2014.

———. S.v. "Tornado Records." December 19, 2014.

FORT WAYNE IS STILL SEVENTH ON HITLER'S LIST

Ankenbruck, John. *Twentieth Century History of Fort Wayne.* Fort Wayne, IN: Twentieth Century Historical Fort Wayne, 1975.

Beatty, John, and Phyllis Robb. *History of Fort Wayne and Allen County, 1700–2005.* Evansville, IN: M. T. Publishing, 2006.

Fort Wayne Civilian Defense Collection, Allen County–Fort Wayne Historical Society.

THE GIRL IN THE SURF

Prescott (Arizona) Courier. "Woman Drowns in Sea." December 6, 1990.

Seftel, Josh, dir. "My Way: Still Life." *This American Life.* Showtime: March 29, 2007.

HIROFUKUSKIMA

Hatchobori Streetcar Survivors. "The Voice of Hibakusha." *Atomic Archive.* National Science Digital Library. Accessed April 11, 2014. http://www.atomicarchive.com/Docs/Hibakusha/Hatchobori.shtml.

Kawamoto, Yoshitaka. "The Voice of Hibakusha." *Atomic Archive.* National Science Digital Library. Accessed April 11,

2014. http://www.atomicarchive.com/Docs/Hibakusha
/Yoshitaka.shtml.

Kita, Isao. "The Voice of Hibakusha." *Atomic Archive*. National
Science Digital Library. Accessed April 11, 2014. http://www
.atomicarchive.com/Docs/Hibakusha/Isao.shtml.

Sakama, Motoko. "Hiroshima's Legacy: The Story of One
Japanese Family." *Christian Science Monitor*. August 2, 1995.
http://www.csmonitor.com/1995/0802/02101.html.

Teremae, Taeko. "The Voice of Hibakusha." *Atomic Archive*.
National Science Digital Library. Accessed April 11, 2014.
http://www.atomicarchive.com/Docs/Hibakusha/Taeko
.shtml.

Wells, W. "Dr. Kaoru Shima: His Recollections of Hiroshima
after the A-Bomb." *American Surgeon* 24, no. 9 (1958).

A TEST OF THE EMERGENCY ALERT SYSTEM

Morton, Jason. "West Ala. Suffers Death, Destruction."
Tuscaloosa News. April 28, 2011.

Taylor, Stephanie. "Tornado Devastates Tuscaloosa." *Tuscaloosa
News,* April 27, 2011.

Tuscaloosa News. "The Aftermath: Staff Accounts of the
Tornado." April 27, 2011.

———. "Survivors Crawl from the Rubble." April 28, 2011.

———. "Tornado Ravages City." April 28, 2011.

CREDITS

The epigraph is from Adrienne Rich's "Diving into the Wreck" © 2013 W. W. Norton & Company.

These essays have appeared in slightly different forms in the following magazines:

"Bedtime Story," *Brain, Child,* 2014

"Buckethead," *Ascent,* 2012

"Death by Refrigerator," *The Normal School,* 2013

"Dispatches from the Drownings," *Mid-American-Review,* 2013

"Epistle to an Embryo" (previously titled "Baby's First Disaster"), *Sonora Review,* 2012

"Fabricating Fear," *The Rumpus,* 2013

"Fifty Ways of Looking at Tornadoes," *Quarterly West,* 2012; reprinted in *Greetings from Duluth* chapbook, Dzanc rEprint Series, 2014

"Fort Wayne Is Still Seventh on Hitler's List," *North American Review,* 2011; reprinted in *Greetings from Duluth* chapbook, Dzanc rEprint Series, 2014

"The Girl in the Surf," *Creative Nonfiction*, 2012

"Goodbye, Tuscaloosa," *TriQuarterly*, 2011

"Hirofukushima," *Passages North*, 2015

"The Longest Wait," *Devil's Lake*, 2012

"Punch Line," *Brevity*, 2014

"A Test of the Emergency Alert System" (previously titled "This Is a Test of the Emergency Alert System"), *The Offending Adam*, 2011

"To the Good People of Joplin," *St. Louis Dispatch, Kansas City Star*, 2011

"The Year of the Great Forgetting," *Hayden's Ferry Review*, 2014

BOOK CLUB GUIDE

1. Throughout these essays, Hollars often relies upon distinctive structures (tests, lists, epistles, enumerations, and parallel narratives, among others) to recount recurring stories in new ways. What is the effect of these distinctive structures? Do they alter your emotional response? Force you to reconsider these events in new ways?

2. In part I, "Dizzied," Hollars often repeats the line "I am trying to write my way out of disaster." How does this repetition reflect on the author's own personal grappling with disasters? Is the repetition a symptom of post-traumatic stress? If so, is writing a means of liberation?

3. In addition to exploring natural disasters, many of Hollars's essays confront disasters of a more personal nature. How do Hollars's essays on fatherhood connect with his essays on natural disasters?

4. Many of Hollars's essays utilize both in-depth research and personal experience. Does one of the two provide more credibility for you? Or rather, how do research and personal experience contribute to the author's credibility in different ways?

5. In essays such as "Goodbye, Tuscaloosa," "The Changing," and "The Year of the Great Forgetting," Hollars examines how we are all at the mercy of our surroundings—that none of us can

ever prepare fully for the uncontrollable hardships of the world. How do these ideas complicate themselves throughout the essays? Does Hollars ever acknowledge the futility of his own efforts as a father incapable of protecting his children against all dangers?

6. The book's title, *This Is Only a Test*, implies that the book's depictions of real-life danger are limited. How do these essays explore authentic danger alongside invented danger? Which of Hollars's fears are real, and which are justified by anxiety?

7. Inherent in many of Hollars's essays are ethical questions: How are we to react while enduring a disaster? What are we to report? What is off-limits? After reading these essays, ask yourself: What are my own views on these questions? Specifically, you might refer to the author's ethical dilemma in "The Girl in the Surf" and juxtapose it with photojournalist Marc Halevi's own ethical dilemma.

8. Both "Fifty Ways of Looking at Tornadoes" and "Dispatches from the Drownings" rely upon numerical lists to incorporate vast amounts of research. To what extent does this simplistic structure succeed in organizing such diverse information? How does the juxtaposition between simplistic structure and complex research speak to the themes expressed therein?

9. In both "Buckethead" and "Death by Refrigerator" Hollars refers to a camp ghost story involving a drowning victim named Bobby Watson. The essays handle the story quite differently. At the start of "Buckethead," the story is presented as fact. Yet in "Death by Refrigerator" Hollars makes clear that the story is most likely fictional. How do these alternative views affect your reading experience? Do you trust Hollars less or more as a result of his offering various perspectives? More broadly, what do these different versions tell us about mythmaking in general?

10. In "Fort Wayne Is Still Seventh on Hitler's List," Hollars shares the story of a city's coming to terms with its allegedly impending destruction. Though Hitler never bombed the city of Fort Wayne, the mere speculation that he might was enough to drive the city to action. People speak often of being "frozen by fear," but in what ways might fear serve to mobilize us in common cause?

11. In "Hirofukushima," Hollars pairs the parallel narratives of the bombing of Hiroshima in 1945 and the Fukushima Daiichi nuclear disaster of 2011. Despite the more than sixty years that separate the events, they are wedded together by the destruction of radiation. However, what separates the stories is intent. While the United States purposefully dropped the atomic bomb in wartime, the Fukushima Daiichi nuclear disaster was a result of human error. Do these differences in intent change your feelings toward either event? Does Hollars's use of juxtaposition complicate your feelings? If so, how?

12. Throughout the collection, Hollars often relies upon the epistle form to directly address a specific audience ("Epistle to an Embryo," "To the Good People of Joplin," "Bedtime Story"). How do these more directed essays speak to you, particularly since you are not part of the named audience? Does this create a sense of voyeurism? A breached intimacy?

13. While natural disasters often strip us of all control, writing an essay is dependent upon the writer's control. How might writing serve as a response to a natural disaster?

14. As the essay collection progresses, so, too, does Hollars's experience as a father. How does the author mature along with these disasters, both those endured and those observed? Does the writing change with the author's maturation?

15. "A Test of the Emergency Alert System" ends with an essay question and three lined pages. Take a moment to try to answer the essay question. How might you respond to Hollars's questions (which, in truth, are less questions than another outlet for the author to express his own fears)? Nevertheless, how will you fill those pages? What disasters have you endured? How might your words serve as your liberation?

B. J. HOLLARS is author of two award-winning nonfiction books—*Thirteen Loops: Race, Violence, and the Last Lynching in America* and *Opening the Doors: The Desegregation of the University of Alabama and the Fight for Civil Rights in Tuscaloosa*—as well as a collection of stories, *Sightings* (IUP, 2013). His hybrid text, *Dispatches from the Drownings: Reporting the Fiction of Nonfiction* was published in the fall of 2014. An Assistant Professor of English at the University of Wisconsin–Eau Claire, he lives a simple existence with his wife, their children, and their dog.

CPSIA information can be obtained at www.ICGtesting.com
Printed in the USA
LVOW11s1954030216

473535LV00005B/155/P

ML 2/16